Pilgrimages

Pilgrimages: Memories of Colonial Macau and Hong Kong

Maria N. Ng

香港大學出版社
HONG KONG UNIVERSITY PRESS

Hong Kong University Press
14/F Hing Wai Centre
7 Tin Wan Praya Road
Aberdeen
Hong Kong

© Hong Kong University Press 2009

Hardback   ISBN 978-962-209-081-1
Paperback   ISBN 978-962-209-208-2

Secure On-line Ordering
http://www.hkupress.org

British Library Cataloguing-in-Publication Data
A catalogue record for this book is available from the British Library.

Printed and bound by Condor Production Co. Ltd., Hong Kong, China

Contents

Acknowledgements

This memoir project was made possible by a generous Canada Council for the Arts Grant for Professional Writers in 2005, which enabled me to travel to Hong Kong for research. I also want to thank the University of Lethbridge for a research grant that facilitated my research trip to Porto in 2004, and a study leave in 2006 that allowed me to finish writing the manuscript. Sneja Gunew kindly invited me to spend my study leave at the Centre for Women's and Gender Studies, UBC. Briana Struss patiently proofread my writing. Julia Kuehn invited me to her Hong Kong apartment to show me how expats live in Hong Kong today. Colin Day introduced me to the Foreign Correspondents' Club. Last but not least, Charles Moorhead helped me analyze and read architecture, provided me with the space to write, and as always, gave me encouragement and support.

Note on appendix

"An Academic Insertion" appears in an original version "Mapping the Diasporic Self" in *Canadian Literature* #196 (Spring 2008): 34–45. I would like to thank *Canadian Literature* for allowing an amended version to appear in this book.

Preface

I have not always kept a diary, so many things I write depend on memories.

I didn't have an extraordinary life — no war, no famine, no earthquake, and so on. But I was born in an extraordinary city and grew up in another equally extraordinary one. These places shape my life; they continue to instil in me the kind of meditativeness so necessary for a literary life. Since I spent over twenty years as, in a way, "guest" of these two cities, feeling at home and also not at home has become a state of natural being. Now, I travel at least six times, usually more, a year, going from the place I work to the place I write; going from one conference to another; visiting one university lecture hall followed by another. Going back to Hong Kong now, I would feel no less a visitor than if I were going for a brief stay in Germany. Going back to the place I work from wherever I have been means the slow beginning of another departure. The first minutes of waking up in a city that is not one's home bring surprise — (*Why is the morning so bright? Where is the roar of traffic coming from?*), as well as sweet familiarity — (*Great, I am en route! Wonderful, I have to start negotiating different social relationships! Ah, what language should I use or can I use today?*).

This book is about British Hong Kong, as well as Portuguese Macau, two colonial outposts during the first two decades of my life. It's also a record of uprootedness, of living through memories while experiencing the present intensely. I feel a strong urge to imitate Lawrence Durrell's rapturous evocation of hot and teeming Alexandria when I write about Macau, though I spent the majority of my youth in Hong Kong. Perhaps it's because Macau, my birthplace, was exotic to me while Hong Kong was where I lived and went to school. Perhaps I was grateful that the Portuguese government was willing to grant me citizenship while the British government treated most Hong Kong Chinese as second-class people, not worthy of a British passport. Or perhaps it's because the Portuguese have lived in Macau for a much longer period of time than the British in Hong Kong, and the Iberian colonizers have assimilated the Chinese culture and vice versa, so that Macanese culture is distinctly Macanese, while in Hong Kong, the British kept aloof from the Chinese multitude and the Chinese culture.

I have so much more affection for Portugal that when I visited the country, it felt like home, ridiculous as it might be — I could imagine living there. The rocky landscape of northern Portugal, the glimmering river leading out to the ocean, the heat in Lisboa that covers like a blanket, the blue and yellow tiles in the railway station — it was all familiar. It's entirely appropriate, to my mind, to begin my journey back with my imagined mother country. When I visited England (which would be appalled if I should call it my mother country), the first time in the 70s, the English people, the cabs, Buckingham Palace, the Mall, Harrods — all reinforced the belief that was inculcated in me since childhood that English culture was superior in a colonial way. England was exciting but also not my home country. Of course, I am not naïve enough to believe that I could integrate into Portuguese society and be accepted as a Portuguese. But emotionally and psychologically, it is much more congenial to me.

Ultimately, this book is really about the two cities, separated from each other by the Pearl River Delta, during the last decades of colonial culture when I was growing up, and only incidentally, about me.

Much could have changed since the time of writing. Such is the dynamic nature of Hong Kong, and to a lesser degree, Macau.

Introduction:
Life Writing and Borderlands

I teach and research cultural studies, an area that, in Ien Ang's analysis, "conceives of itself as a borderland formation, an open-ended and multivocal discursive formation." Certainly, the implied transcultural and transnational nature of intellectual borderlands appeals greatly to someone who grew up in one culture and nation and works in another culture and carries a different passport. Furthermore, borderland existence, to borrow Ang's term, promises liberation from a past perceived as burdened with the inauthentic baggage of colonial acculturation. Thus, I experience borderland existence both geographically and metaphorically. However, this liberation is short-lived when I start writing a memoir of my childhood and teenage years in Hong Kong, when past and present confront each other not as a series of teleological events but as territorial conflicts. Persistently, my impulse to write as-I-know-it is curbed by either a lack of architectural and physical evidence, or by finding my knowledge negated by another witness. The emotional need to "write back," if not postcolonially to the metropolitan centre, then to some personal psychological repository, is frequently checked by the life-long training of writing rationally. And I am forcibly struck by the irony that a postcolonialist should find herself indulging in a nostalgic journey to a lost colonial past. Life writing, then, as practised by an academic, becomes an anxiety-ridden borderland existence as one confronts one's past, a practice often giving the impression of slipping out of the control of intellectual debates and discussions.

Much of my present intellectual profile has been shaped by specific Hong Kong places in my youth, which I had considered to be a suitable starting point for recalling my early life. First and foremost is the Catholic convent I attended. Like other writers (for example, Edna O'Brien, Jean Rhys, Simone de Beauvoir), I find growing up under the influence of nuns and the rituals of the Catholic church of primal importance in my life. I am partial to clothes that have a flowing shape because they remind me of the habit of the nuns. I prefer the combination of black and white because, for years, those were the colours worn by my teachers. I enjoy choral music because we listened to it every morning at assembly. The sense of guilt and the need for perpetual redemption have been indelibly ingrained in me. The ideal preparation to write my memoir would be to go back to the convent and experience a day-in-the-life-of again, in order to rediscover and reassess what growing up in a convent would be like from an adult perspective. Sadly, though the building is still there, it has been sold to some private and secular educational enterprise. No nuns, no morning assembly, no Wednesday-afternoon chapel, no Latin mass.

Apart from the convent library, I learned to love reading at two colonial outposts in Hong Kong in the 60s — the United States Information Service and the British Council Reading Room. In my memoir, I dwell with great affection on these places. They provided a sanctuary for a young girl who needed an escape — from family obligations, from the Chinese culture that she was alienated from because of her colonial and convent education, from a general philistine culture of trade that energized the city. In my memory, the books in the libraries blocked out the noise and reality from the outside world the way the cork-lined walls protected Proust as he sat in his bed to write. I took no pictures of these places, but I remember them well and with affection. Both libraries have been gone since the 90s or earlier. They might exist in other forms in the age of the internet; but gone are the rooms lined with book shelves and furnished with refectory tables and green-shaded lamps. How much, then, are these affectionate pictures a form of nostalgic indulgence, since I do not even have an existing architectural structure to compare them with?

As if finding no architectural witness to my memory were not enough to undermine my will to recall, my mother, the only living witness to my childhood, disagreed with me on certain key moments when we discussed them. My mother is in her eighties. Would her memory be more reliable than mine? Yet her collaboration would be welcomed and useful. Neither of us kept a diary. We have no written record to resort to as arbitrator. I decide to trust myself rather than her.

I don't trust my mother's memory; I find it harder to write about her. But how can one's memoir be complete without an analysis of the effect one's mother has on one? I wrote an essay on representations of the mother figure by ethnic Chinese writers. In it, I argue that it is much easier to analyze one's mother if one writes in a language that is not the "mother" tongue, and even easier if one's mother cannot access the language in which the criticism is published. Thus, it should be easy for me to write about my mother, since I am not writing in Chinese and my mother will not be able to read the English text.

So what is hindering me from putting my life-long evaluation of my mother on paper? In John D. Barbour's essay, "Judging and Not Judging Parent," he suggests that being a parent might make a writer realize "how difficult it is to be a good parent, and therefore may make one more understanding or forgiving of a father or mother." I agree that being a parent oneself might provide insight into parenting, but I disagree that this insight should in any way stand in the way of evaluating one's parent. Perhaps I am putting too much faith in the trained academic's ability to remain objective. Yet if one is engaged in critical assessment, then experiencing what the object of the critical assessment, in this case one's parent, might once have experienced should not be an obstacle. One does not stop "panning" books just because one realizes that it is indeed difficult to write books. Similarly, a prosecuting lawyer does not stop prosecuting even though she notices in herself the same failings that are evident in the person being prosecuted.

In my case, the reluctance is a result of conflicting cultural influences and less a matter of experiential empathy. My Western education has inculcated in me, from the very first class exercise in explication and the first analytical essay, the habit of looking at people and situations objectively, even if they might be one's relations and the situations are personal ones. Thus, as soon as I have attained the faculty of critical analysis (as a teenager), I have both reacted emotionally to my mother and also analyzed her actions and decisions as if we were part of an anthropological project. Though I would not necessarily subscribe to Freud's theory that mother and daughter are engaged in sexual rivalry, I admit that the relationship between my mother and me is often tense. As an intellectual and as a daughter, I was and still am perpetually crossing and re-crossing the terrain of the trained academic and the emotional domain of a daughter resenting her mother for reasons that have been too well documented.

While my Western education provides me with the belief (or illusion?) that any personal bias could be overcome by intellectual analysis, my Chinese background teaches blind adherence to principles that could be traced back to the third century B.C. One of the most important and immutable principles in Confucianist teaching, to which all Chinese children are exposed, at home or at school, is that which concerns one's parents. The concept of filial piety is, as I admit in an academic essay on the subject of the mother, "an inalienable part of all ethnic Chinese subjectivities." Not only is one taught to respect, but one is led to believe that one must never refuse what is due to one's parents: unquestioning obedience, which is the opposite of the critical and individual mind so valued by Western education. This internalized belief that I owe everything to my parents, and that I should spend my life repaying this debt, unfortunately, coincides with the Catholic sense of guilt cultivated in me during my convent years, resulting in paralysis when I have to address the section in my life that deals with my mother.

While planning to write about my mother, I also consider the ethical aspect articulated in G. Thomas Couser's *Ethics and Life Writing*. Using John Bayley's *Elegy for Iris* as an example, Couser reminds the reader that "[i]n depicting his demented wife, Bayley is representing someone I would describe as a vulnerable subject." To Couser, Murdoch was both unaware of being represented and "without competence to consent to having her dementia so publicly portrayed." My mother is not mentally incompetent; but she is vulnerable in other ways. She cannot defend herself against any criticism levelled at her because of her educational background and her linguistic limitation. Having only achieved the equivalent of primary school education, my mother does not have the analytical training to express her emotions and thoughts in an articulate manner. One of the causes of our frequent disputes centres on her purely instinctive reactions to experience as opposed to mine as outlined above. It will be impossible to make her understand that what I attempt to do is not an act of betrayal and a gross transgression of what is acceptable filial behaviour. Furthermore, my mother does not have the linguistic ability to read what I might write about her; thus she cannot defend my representation of her and our lives together.

Yet, I can say with all honesty that the manner in which I was brought up, acceptable in Chinese culture, would have been considered mildly abusive and questionable in Western culture. Public and verbal humiliation, relentless disciplining, physical punishment — those were all part of the family regime. I don't know the reason for my mother's ferocious need to assert her authority over her only daughter, but this need had virtually crippled me psychologically throughout my childhood and early adulthood. Thus, I also have to question my own motive: is it an act of personal revenge to write about my mother, or am I trying to speak for the many Chinese who have experienced similar familial oppression and repressions?

It is ironic that the impetus to write critically is a result of the education my parents chose for me. While xenophobic with regards to the colonial presence in Hong Kong, my parents did not question the ways the nuns were going to shape my intellect. (Friendship with non-Chinese was not only frowned upon but interdict when I was growing up. At least, that was my memory.) Because of this Western education of liberal humanism, I have developed the intellectual apparatus to question authority, history, and racial hierarchy, which ultimately leads to studying postcolonial culture and writing. In this way, my multiple-subjectivities and multiple-affiliations provide not only the metaphorical borderland existence Ang discusses, they also result in the actual geographical crossing and re-crossing necessitated by family obligations, emigration/immigration, and academic research.

Each time I revisit Hong Kong, I see it with a postcolonial lens: the physical remnants of colonial rule, the leftovers of colonial privileges, the marginalization of expat communities that used to be the cultural dominant and so on. But preparing and writing my memoir, based on my pre-emigrant life, my life as a Chinese living in Hong Kong, and my happy days at a convent school, was all about being part of the colonial culture. I can manage this borderland anxiety in various ways. The first is to take up an ideological position as a postcolonialist committed to criticize all that was colonial in my life. I can also rearrange materials so that the Chinese side of my Hong Kong life is privileged and the positive effects of the colonial aspects diminished. Or I can take this project as a challenge, not only a personal one, but also one that interrogates the interstitial space that must have been encountered by many others in the age of mobility and shifting national identities. Maybe I can also turn the project into an attempt at voicing experiences for those who have, like me, an ambivalent colonial upbringing that is not so easily categorized and contained within ready-made theoretical frameworks. This can also be a project that articulates the borderlands not only as some "utopian site of transgressive intermixture, hybridity and multiplicity," according to Ien Ang, but also as a site of concrete and metaphorical examinations and negotiations. Finally, I should embrace borderland existence as part of my reality and write about it.

At first, I intended my early life narrative to be patterned on the classic *Bildungsroman* — a structure based on chronological developments. But I don't recall my childhood linearly; I see snapshots and remember situations. It was a revelation to read that Margaret Laurence, as Helen Buss reports, didn't want to structure her memoir, *Dance on the Earth* (1989) in novelistic form; that "'pages and pages' of chronological narrative [...] left her 'bored silly'." Liberated from the tyranny of narrating one's life in logical sequences and vastly impressed by Orhan Pamuk's *Istanbul*, at once a memoir and a record of a place, I map out my early life in segments that could be comparable to a series of pictures of a journey, but not an itinerary married to time and dates necessarily. Again, this structure seems to fit in well with the idea that writing memoirs is an act of living in borderlands. Remembering and writing and revising involve movements, interior and exterior, metaphorical and practical. Remembering and writing also entail story telling.

I have a strong desire to romanticize my memories; but, as an academic, I have been trained to be honest in dealing with ideas and words. Every scenario is a result of rhetorical hesitation, self-examination, and reluctance. In the Macau section, I solve the problem of narrative veracity against narrative fancifulness by inserting fictional conversations and events, in order to highlight the difference between a life lived and the life imagined. I also ground my narrative in places. The narrator might veer from truth, however inadvertently; but the places existed and some continue to exist. The first section "Porto" is an illustration of how I try to narrate through place. My memoir does not begin at the beginning. Nor does it begin with my birthplace. It begins with a journey I took to Portugal in 2004, in search of a cultural past that has nothing to do with my ethnic origin. I want to tell the reader that this is not a classical kind of memoir narrative.

Porto

A Pilgrim to Porto

Fado singing actually sounded quite like Cantonese opera, I told myself as the train raced through the hilly countryside of Spain towards northern Portugal. Like José Saramago, I thought of myself as a pilgrim and a traveller, not a tourist. Like all pilgrims, I believed that I had a special relationship with the place I was visiting. There are invisible ties between Portugal and myself, not at all apparent to outsiders.

My birth certificate (*Assentos de Nascimento*), my identity card (*Bilhete de Identidade*), my fingerprints and other essential data are stored at a place called *Conservatória dos Registos Centrais* in Lisbon. Childhood, to me, was images of an esplanade called Rua de Praia Grande, palm trees and lush gardens, pink villas and yellow baroque churches. My Macanese childhood made me feel much closer to Portugal than to the small towns in Southern China, where my parents and their parents came from. Which explains why in late June, a Chinese woman got up at five in the morning as the sleeper train crossed the line between Spain and Portugal. I wanted to be awake at this moment. I tried to identify the countryside, but all I could see was the sun coming up behind the hills. Still, I said to myself, "I am home."

Having read Saramago's *Journey to Portugal*, I was prepared for a country of stark landscape and hardworking people. There were olives trees, and sheep, and rough stone huts. There were little towns with shuttered storefronts and buildings that needed a new coat of paint but looked as if they didn't care. My romantic heart sank; I hoped that as the train pulled closer to Porto, the landscape would change. It did.

Before reaching Porto, the train stopped at oceanfront towns such as Esinho, where women hung colourful laundry on lines that ran parallel to the train tracks. And pizza takeouts. And video rentals. Portuguese towns looked not dissimilar from other suburbs around the world. By then, I was desperate for something evocatively Portuguese. Luckily, for a traveller hungry for "authentic" Portugal, there was nothing more satisfying than to step off the train and walk into the waiting hall of Sao Bento station. Quite a small station, built in 1900, its walls were covered by 20,000 tiles (so the guidebook told me), in the best *azulejos* (painted ceramic tiles) tradition. Sao Bento was not an ultra modern station. It belonged to a different era, with its ornate but faded décor and travellers dressed in drab but functional clothes. There were no fast-food outlets, no insurance kiosks, no Relay bookstores. I was too tired, after nineteen hours on the train, to take in the significance of the tiles. But I was thankful that my first sight of Porto was a scene so intensely Portuguese and so unlike a generic, international train station.

The hotel, located on the main street Avenida dos Aliados, was a turn-of-last-century affair. Dignified, ornate, but without fanfare. One walked up to the second floor where the reception desk was, and saw beyond, down a narrow corridor, the hotel sitting room for guests, with red plush sofas and antimacassars and aspidistras. Not unlike a sitting room one would find in a seaside hotel decades ago in England. I remembered living rooms like this in Macau too. Imported decors from colonialists. Later, when I explored the various corridors on the floor where my room was, I found one service stairwell and was enchanted to see white bed sheets hanging on rods to air dry. Who was washing these sheets? The shy woman who dusted the side tables with the plastic vases of flowers?

Lacking a proper map of Porto, I went to the street indicated as the shopping street, Rua de Santa Catarina, where I found a small but packed bookshop just about to close for the weekend. Like many other shops on this and other streets in Porto, this unpretentious store had an Art Nouveau storefront of cast iron and glass worthy of Otto Wagner. The young woman spoke English well enough to show me where the maps were. She even tried to help me find books on Macau. We found none. Obviously, this former colony didn't play a major role when the buyer ordered books for the store. This was the first indication that my love affair with Portugal was pretty one-sided.

River Life

Like all major cities, the most vibrant urban scenes in Porto took place near the river. One walked from the city centre down steep narrow streets to the Ribiera, a colourful and nonchalant jumble by the river Douro. One passed dark doorways, dusty shop windows, Porto citizens sitting on door stoops chatting the evening away. Lower-middle-class Portuguese taking their time over telling an anecdote, the flickering of television just visible in the back of a doorway propped up by two men in their undershirts and baggy trousers. Unabashedly frilly bed linen hung from the windows. Some beggar woman aggressively tugged at one's arm, showing off her baby. I didn't know what she was saying, but could guess that money was needed for feeding the baby. I shook my head — I had seen too many of them in the city square and around the train station already.

Children diving off the wharf to show off to tourists; well-baked English or Germans stood around, somewhat nonplussed — the vibrant heat and the helter-skelter kiosks that sold souvenirs or beer or Portuguese flags were confusing to them. Noise, a lot of noise. Crowds, a lot of people. I found a small, seedy restaurant — more like a take-out — and sat on the patio. The beer was cheaper than the busier places; the choices on the menu were few. I sat and watched as an old woman packed up her folding table of postcards and Portuguese football scarves, since no one was buying anything from her.

She was overweight; she was at least seventy-five, though Portuguese could look older than their actual age; she was dressed in a way that I had only read about — a kind of voluminous long dress with an apron over it; she had stiff joints and staggered a bit as she tried to carry her table into one of many narrow corridors that led mysteriously into the interior of an apartment building. I leaned over to try and catch a glimpse of the inside and only saw carton boxes and broken household items stacked haphazardly against the wall. I couldn't tell if this was a sign of poverty or just the Porto way of dealing with one's possessions. But the sight of this grandmother, many years past retirement age in G-7 countries, trying to eke out a living, or allowance, smack in the middle of a tourist neighbourhood, told me that Porto didn't try to smarten everything up just for the pernickety taste of well-heeled visitors.

The riverfront was divided into different districts. Not much happened along the Migragaia, but one could take a tram that would travel along the river all the way to Foz Velha, where the Douro joined the Atlantic Ocean. Unlike the Ribiera, the Foz was eerily deserted, even on a hot sunny afternoon. Someone told me that the water here was frigid. The Praça Gonçalves Zarco was a cold, white, windswept, empty space. It was hard to imagine what the town planners had in mind. I walked from garage to underpass back to echoing garage, getting lost while trying to get from the waterfront to the Avenida da Boavista, where I could see the awning of a single restaurant in a long and wide boulevard.

In contrast, if one turned away from Boavista, which would take one to modern shopping malls, and walked along Avenida de Montevideu, all the way to Avenida do Brasil, one could stop at ice-cream trucks, toyshops, clothing boutiques, quayside beer huts. The esplanade reminded me of the ones back in Macau, lined with palm trees and utterly spectacular because one knew one was walking on the edge of the ocean.

Church Scenes

I grew up in churches. My earliest memory of architecture is still that of Santa Rosa Convent in Macau, a sprawling stone building set in a tropical garden. So, naturally, I was drawn to the churches in Porto. The Sé, the cathedral, was impressive by its very location, set atop the cliffside of Porto, a majestically dour building that looked on as river life flowed by. One could take a gondola ride up the steep cliff from the Ribiera to reach the cathedral square. Or one could do penance for the vacation diet of overeating and walk up the steps. I believe Saramago counted them. Sitting next to the Sé was the Bishops' Palace. I peered inside the vestibule — no visitors allowed — and saw a cavernous, cool, shadowed hall, of dark stone and narrow windows. Leaning over the parapet of the square, I looked down into the tranquil garden of what appeared to be a seminary — palm trees, blue and white tiles, tropical plants in clay pots, shuttered windows behind filigree iron grills against the afternoon sun. Children were jumping in and out of a fountain hewn from the cliffside.

On Sunday, I walked along Rua de Santa Catarina and witnessed the potential clashing of two groups of devotees. From a parish church exited Porto citizens who had just attended the nine o'clock mass. From the underground parking of a shopping centre debouched a group of visiting football fans, loud in their costumes and in their hearty singing. In the hands of the churchgoers were missals and rosaries. In the hands of the football fans were plastic mugs of beer. The fans marched down the middle of Santa Catarina shouting their club song while the devout Portuguese looked on, bemused and tolerant. There was no incident and the police were not involved.

Although all guidebooks would urge the traveller to visit S. Francisco, less for architectural merits and more for its overkill in gold ornamentation, the quieter and poorer churches, I found, were rewarding for reasons that perhaps only a Macanese would understand. In Macau, churches built by the colonizers were everywhere; some were as old as those in Porto. Like the Porto churches, those in the former colony were run down, lacking in upkeep, seedy but still impressive in their faded beauty. They weren't meant for the tourist trade, but for the local believers and petitioners. Candles flickered in the dim interior; pews worn from years of kneeling; a patch of wood on the door was smoothed from countless hands pushing it open. I placed my hand on the same patch and pushed and was startled by the daylight outside.

Bookshops

The guidebook said the must-see bookstore was called Livraria Lello.
The receipt I got said it was called Prologo. Whatever its name, it was
a magnificent bookstore, even surpassing one housed in a baroque
building I visited in Florence. The exterior of Prologo was neo-Gothic
in its ornateness, matched by the Art Nouveau intricacies of its interior.
On the ground floor, a minicart ran along a rail that allowed the staff to
move books back and forth. The grand staircase branched out on the
mezzanine in curves and foliage, ending on the second floor that was
coffered by a stained glass ceiling. I found Rose Macaulay's classic,
They Went to Portugal, but at 56 euros, it was far too expensive. Instead,
I bought a history of Portugal in Portuguese, thus impressing the
manager, who handed me his business card with a courtly flourish. But
when he started speaking to me, I had to admit that I didn't really know
the language. I asked for books on Macau. No, Prologo didn't have any
books on Macau.

I found the address of Livraria Leitura in the phone book. It was in
a modern building on Rua de Ceuta. In the distance, one could see a
piece of the original medieval city wall with apartments built abutting
it. Leitura consisted of several rooms connected by narrow passages. I
went into the history, literature, and philosophy room and after spending
time looking at books on Derrida and Marx, I asked the assistant if the
bookstore had books on Macau. She took me to a shelf and indeed, I
found more than a dozen titles. She helped me carry them to a coffee
table and I sat down to go leisurely through each of them. Leitura had
no problem arranging to ship the ones I selected to Canada, and after
deciding on the postage charges, the assistant gave me a written receipt
and asked me to pay at the cashier. (When the books arrived after two
weeks, they were wrapped in brown paper and tied with a string; the
address was handwritten in ink. I couldn't bear to unwrap a package
that showed such signs of the human touch.)

Morning

After a week in Porto, I found that, while it resonated with my childhood memories, its culture was also alien and alienating. Perhaps I had spent too much time in Canada. The sights of old people working, the use of children by beggars, the religious fervour that was palpable. I was surprised to find a totally dilapidated building in the city centre, an invitation to squatters. I shrank from the raucous cries of street people who seemed theatrically angry. I gawked at the dusty and soiled window displays of religious artefacts in numerous shops. I wondered if anyone actually bought the antimacassars that had turned yellow and whose edges were curled from age. Porto shops sold things that I didn't think existed anymore in Western societies.

But the heat, the palm trees, the flaking baroque churches, the river that ran into the ocean — they spoke to me.

On the last morning of my stay, I leaned out of the balcony of the hotel room and looked down at the streets. It was seven and some people were on their way to work, dressed in no-nonsense greys and whites. The building next door was a bank, with marble front steps and tiled sidewalks. An older woman, in a faded floral dress and apron, was on her knees scrubbing the steps methodically, painstakingly, slowly. I followed her arched back, her genuflections, her sweeping arm movements. I had only read about housemaid knees but I wouldn't be surprised if this cleaning woman had them. She wasn't an immigrant from one of Portugal's former colonies. She was a Portuguese, and like many Portuguese, she worked hard to make a living and to keep the city functioning. I was oddly moved and immensely impressed by this faceless woman. In many ways, she was not unlike the people in Macau I remembered.

The hillside of Porto, Portugal

The Livraria Lello in Porto

A cleaning woman at dawn in Porto

Macau

The Coming of the Portuguese

Last night I dreamt of Vasco da Gama again. In my dream, I was not transported back to the sixteenth century, sailing across the restless oceans as Camoens tells us in *The Lusiad*. In my dream, da Gama wore a two-day stubble, dark against a strong jawline and framing a face with high cheekbones. He walked beside me, silently, along the Rua da Praia Grande, occasionally looking out at the bay, at a landscape changed and defaced by constructions of one kind or another. In my dream, we were in Macau, the Macau of the twentieth-first century.

I never understand why I should have such fantastic dreams. After all, nothing is more unlike the former sub-tropical Portuguese colony than the Canadian prairies that I call home now. The Macau of my childhood was all curves and slight undulation. The town I live and work in is flat. Flat with a fierce determination I find totally depressing. Macau was warm; one would quietly, secretly, perspire in the dark nights. The prairie winters are cold; cold and bright in the day, cold and not so bright in the night. Not velvet-like, a prairie night has a starched and stiff quality that is unnerving.

No wonder I dream of the tropics.

One always wants to be somewhere else. The condition of an immigrant. The condition of a postmodern immigrant. Growing up in the tropics has taught me that. The heat, the noise, the swarming colours — they had but one lesson: go away; go away and then suffer eternal homesickness. One never enjoys the heat when it is 33 degrees Celsius in the shade. Nor the competing smell of ripening fruits — the mangoes and the pineapples and the peaches and the dragon-eyes. The flowers look provocatively garish — flushing pink bougainvillea, creamy gardenia, red clusters of azalea. And the sweat drying on people's skin — it is pervasive; it penetrates everything unless one keeps only to air-conditioned spaces; its acridity eats into one's subconscious.

But in my dreams, and there are many, many, I always search for these sensory memories. Rolled up tightly in my functional duvet, I want heat, heat so hot that I perspire, and perspiration would course down my face, along my nose, down the sides of my cheeks, stay like a pool in the hollow of my collar bones, and finally dried, salty, on my chest.

I cannot breathe in the cold, I would say to myself as I curl my toes inside heavy socks, the temperature dipping below minus 20 degrees, making my first coffee and looking out at a bleak winter morning. This heat deprivation might explain the intense nostalgic nature of my memories of the 50s and 60s.

I had rejected the history of Macau when I left the tiny colony for Hong Kong. I thought, in my youthful knowingness, that it was a fake culture (as if Hong Kong had a genuine culture when I was growing up). Macau's language was Portuguese, which I didn't study in school, even though one colony was only two hours' ferry ride from the other. I studied Chinese and English, and thought nothing of the gutturals and slow slurring sounds of the official tongue in Macau. I turned my eyes from the bright blue tiles that lined the walls of some buildings, like the Leal Senado, and ignored the colourful mosaics as I crossed the Largo do Senado, the main square of the city that was patterned on one in Lisboa. I came from generations of Chinese who had originally found refuge in Macau and Hong Kong from the civil unrest in China and then from the invading Japanese. The roots were deep but the loyalties were confused. (The phenomenon of cultural root formation, regardless of race and ethnic affiliations, is a vexatious but rich area of research.)

In the illustration in the book I took out from the library, Vasco da Gama has a hooked nose and rather deep-set eyes. He stands with his legs apart, knees slightly bent, no doubt because he was first and foremost a sailor. Gama was born in 1469, in a southern Atlantic port of Portugal, under the reign of Afonso V, the nephew of Prince Henry, who himself was a grandson of John of Lancaster, whose line eventually founded the Tudor dynasty. In the illustration, Vasco da Gama shows that the Iberian Peninsula in the sixteenth century was as prosperous and sophisticated a place as Tudor England. The explorer is dressed in richly embroidered clothes, his canions and hose are slashed, the puffed sleeves of his jerkin show in swells of intricate stitching underneath the mantle. A heavy chain with a cross lies across his chest. His head is covered in a hat with a turned-up brim, ostrich feathers flowing over its edge. He looks like a suitably flamboyant conqueror of the tropical countries of Asia.

When the future Henry VII of England was engaged in the famous Battle of Bosworth, Gama would have been sixteen years old.

I scan the pages and cross-check another reference book on European history to see what else was happening when Gama, Portugal's most famous sailor, the one-time Viceroy of Estado da India, a fidalgo of the household of the King and a knight of the Order of Santiago, whose voyages made possible the fame of his followers, the Portuguese who travelled and lived and immortalized and plundered the Orient, de Castro, Xavier, Pinto, Camoens ..., was still a teenager.

In Italy, Michaelangelo, Botticelli, Titian. In Germany, Dürer, Grünwald. In England, the Tudors. I now know about the end of the medieval Hungarian Empire, when someone called Vladislav II of Bohemia effectively began the Habsburg Hungarian reign, which did not end until the end of World War I, by confirming the Habsburg's claim to Hungary. Serendipitously I come across the swallowing up of Serbia and Albania in the 1450s by the Ottoman Empire, the slaughter of the noblemen in the Battle of Kossova, and the conversion to Islam in the Balkan states.

Now we are paying for these events. History always returns. And always memories.

In China, the Ming dynasty. The dragon throne. In Macau, life was uneventful. People fished. They knew nothing of the Portuguese carracks that would be plying the Pearl River delta in the next century, or of the *Sao Gabriel, the Sao Rafael*, and the *Berrio* that would leave Portugal in July 1497, in the hot days of the Iberian coast, and reach the eastern coast of India in 1498. Nor of Camoens, known to Macanese because there is a Camoes Grotto in the Camoes Garden, and next to the garden the Camoes Museum. Although Gama never reached Macau, a monument to honour him stood amongst four canons in a surrounding of leafy trees and quiet narrow streets.

The sea voyages took place five centuries ago. I myself also crossed the ocean, the Pacific, but only three decades ago. I did not sail in a barge, or a caravel. I flew to Vancouver, the port city of Canada's Pacific coast. Not so adventurous as the journey endured by these near-savage men of the fifteenth century. Very hygienic. No scurvy during the short trip of fifteen hours. Several tasteless meals. Four movies, one worse than the other. But the same sense of anticipation. The same sense of fear and exhilaration.

To travel is to risk, to tear oneself away from the quotidian, to throw oneself into a darkness that will evolve into light, when strangeness becomes, gradually, familiarity. When we travel, we are like the warriors of olden days. We say to ourselves: we are not afraid. The plane might explode. We might never arrive. We might catch a disease without cure. We cannot communicate. We lose our ways. We lose our documents. We lose our identities. We are not afraid.

These fifteenth-century sailors and I must have shared similar sensations, I thought as I gently, absent-mindedly fingered the rough cover of the book, remembering my first sighting of the water, the mountains, the houses. But all from above. And Gama? What did he see when he first arrived in Calicut?

Talking to Vasco da Gama

I imagine a conversation between Vasco da Gama and myself, co-existing in some parallel universe, might proceed like this:

– Gama? Do you hear me asking you? Come on, you are wandering away in your mind again.

He turned his head, so marked by a combination of noble features— the heavy brows, the deep-set eyes, the prominent nose, and of a kind of crafty sensuousness in his lips, most noticeable when he attempted to smile.

– Gama, why are you looking away from me? Didn't you like the story I have been telling you?

He stopped walking and leant against the parapet along the Rua da Praia Grande.

– My dear, what story?

(I have to place him in Macau — in imagination, geographical reality can be adapted, surely.)

– About your travels, from the Tagus, down the Atlantic, and on and on.

– It is not a story. It is my life you are trying to make into some kind of nonsense. What do they call it today? A narrative. But my life, it is not a narrative.

He shrugged and placed his beautiful hands, one over the other, on the stone surface.

– Then what is it, if not a narrative?

He turned from the sea and faced the buildings, the ugly and the beautiful ones, the new and the old ones left from the past, a port created by his disciples who followed his exploits and pushed their vessels as far east as the Far East. He gestured with his arm at the view in front of him.

– Is this a narrative, the city where you were born? These broken stones? These dirtied walls?

– Yes, oh yes, Gama, Macau is a narrative.

– Then tell me about it.

– Where should I start?

– Start when you fell in love with me?

– With you?

– You are in love with me, the heroic explorer, aren't you? That's why you dream about me, read about me, write about me, compare yourself to me.

– No, Gama. I'm in love with an idea. With a whole era. With a Zeitgeist.

– Don't use German. Use Portuguese, a more beautiful language.

– But I don't speak Portuguese!

– And you have Portuguese citizenship, without the language?

– Gama, it's the twenty-first century. We can adopt nationalities by immigrating, travelling. I became Portuguese because my mother travelled to Macau when she was pregnant. And she travelled to Macau because my grandmother was living here. Actually, she lived not far from where we are standing now.

– Never mind. Tell me the story, this narrative of Macau.

– All right. But Macau's story is my story too.

– Yes, I would like to know more about you, a Chinese woman who carries a Portuguese passport, something I didn't use when I sailed with my men down the Atlantic and across the Indian Oceans, and who speaks fluent English, but not Portuguese, her mother tongue.

– Mother tongue, what nonsense!

– Without a native language, how do you define yourself, your identity, as a citizen that belongs to a kingdom, or now, what is called a nation?

– Gama, a nation now can have many languages. Canada has French and English, and the First Nations ...

– What are First Nations?

– They are the original people who had been living in Canada before the white men came.

– Ah, yes. Like the Indians.

– Actually, Gama, Indians are called South Asians.

– Hmm ...

– And Macau has several languages — Cantonese, Putonghua, English, Portuguese.

– Not English. No, Macau has always been Portuguese.

– Not anymore, Gama. But I should start my story.

– Yes, your narrative.

– Yes, all right ... These memories are in patches — incomplete. But the details will come back. I know.

Fading Colony

I was born in 1952. The Portuguese had been governing Macau since 1557. It was the oldest colony in East and Southeast Asia, and it remained part of Portugal till the turn of the last century. Till the last day of the year 1999. In Canada I was watching a programme on French television about the parties Macanese were hosting to celebrate the Chinese take-over. I cried. (A very transnational moment: Canada–France–Macau–Portugal–China.) I grew up with the gradual waning of Portuguese control over my birthplace. I thought I despised the Portuguese. Partly it was indoctrination — Hong Kong Chinese thought the Macanese lazy and lacking in the make-money-go-getting attitude. But now, I can only dream about the blue tiles, the yellow walls of the villas on the Penha Hill, the cobblestones in front of the St. Augustine church.

I don't know what happened, but I am living in a past that I didn't particularly value when it was the present …

My parents only lived intermittently in the summer in Macau; they rented an apartment, or a flat, as the British called it. I was to know two colonial cultures. I used to prefer the British to the Portuguese, because Hong Kong was growing, while Portuguese Macau was stagnating. In the 50s, Hong Kong was already overcrowded with countless refugees coming over the borders from China. My parents thought I would be better off staying in quiet Macau with my mother's mother, who was a widow. And grandmother could use the extra money she got for keeping me.

The school I was sent to was, of course, a Catholic convent. Santa Rosa. It was built in the neo-baroque Portuguese style that defined many old buildings in Macau, if the Chinese would leave them be. My favourite part of the convent was the garden. Lush. The entrance leading up to the main building was stepped. The steps were awfully wide and I had to walk between taking each step.

We lived in a colonial house similar to those preserved on Taipa Island. Pastel green trimmed in white. A verandah in front. The bedrooms on the top floor opened out to a balcony that looked onto the South China Sea. The furniture was a mix of traditional Chinese and Portuguese designs. The tables had elaborately carved legs and inlaid tops. The bed had white mosquito netting. In the garden we grew bougainvilleas and palms and hibiscus. A riot of colours framed by the window shutters that protected the rooms from the tropical heat.

The Tropics is a dreamy space. The heat, the sun, the blue sky, the steaming pavement. The green of the trees. The red of the flowers. People half naked because of the 35 degrees Celsius. People sweating because of the 35 degrees Celsius. The cool tiles. The green and yellow of the colonial houses. Rua da Barra. Avenida da Praia Grande. Estrada de Adolfo Loureiro. One sat in a square and daydreamed. One sat in a café and sipped ice tea and daydreamed. One walked past Angolan sentries at the Governor's House and thought about Africa. One wandered along the Praia and saw Chinese junks and thought about China. Dishes in restaurants with recipes from Brazil, from Mozambique, from Angola, from China, from Hong Kong.

That's why now, I dream.

Let us say that the above would be a creative re-imagining of my early childhood.

It is true that I was born in Macau. My mother, apparently, decided to give birth near her mother. I never asked about the details of my birth — it seems very unimportant overall. But my Macanese birth was not disputable — I have a birth certificate, now in Lisboa, and baptism certificate, also in Lisboa, to prove my "national" and religious identities. I also lived in Macau for a little while, then went back quite often during the summer holidays, because my grandmother stayed in Macau with her brood until the mid 50s, and both my parents had Macanese friends they met during the war.

My grandmother was an illiterate woman who had many children. That was not an unusual circumstance — Chinese women didn't receive much education, if at all, in the beginning of the twentieth century. If she were rich, she could expect to marry wealthy. If she were poor, as my grandmother was, then she needed to spend her energy and time to help the family, not reading and writing. Her husband, my grandfather, whom I never saw, not even in a picture, was a fighter pilot who studied in Paris, very rare for a Chinese man in those days, early in the century. (But no one seems to know what he studied.) He became an opium addict, unfortunately not such a rare occurrence in China at that time. He wore a white silk scarf, a kind of personal signature. But apart from making my grandmother pregnant regularly, he did nothing for the family. (My grandmother told me these tidbits when I was staying with her in Hong Kong in the late 50s. I believed her then, but knowing what I do now of narrative fabrications, who knows?) Whom did he fight for? China, of course. He died fighting the Japanese, even before World War II. One of his sons also died, during the war, though just by walking past a Japanese sentry in Hong Kong at the wrong time or perhaps, in the wrong manner. The Japanese were the reason why my grandmother lived in Macau and why I was born in Macau. Maybe I should be grateful to them, in an ironic way.

I don't remember anything of my grandmother in Macau, so I depend on my mother as my informant. That in itself is tricky, since my mother had a problematic relationship with her own mother. Being the eldest daughter, much responsibility evolved upon my mother, to help feed the family, to help look after the children and so on. When my mom grew up, she realized that her mother was more partial to the younger children. (I don't blame her for her resentment. Parents are not the fairest and wisest people in the world, and it's a wonder that humanity survives all the mistakes parents make in regard to the bringing up of children.) As far as my own situation is concerned, my mother resented her mother and this resentment was quite obvious to me, which alerted me, at a very young age, to the possibility that a mother-daughter relationship was not a generally happy affair. I don't know how much my mother's bitterness and frustration as a daughter affected the way she treated me — with maximum control; but certainly I was at the receiving end of three generations of unhappy and unsuccessful mother-daughter relationships.

My grandmother moved to Macau in the 40s because it was cheaper to live there and it was away from the turmoil in China, between the

Nationalists and the Communists, between the Chinese and the Japanese. Macau was not strategic. A backwater. No one cared about it then. It became a place of refuge for homeless Chinese, nervous Chinese with wealth, ne'er-do-well colonials from Hong Kong, left-overs from Portugal. It was a place for budding Joseph Conrads and Somerset Maughams. Conrad's Jim would have sought exile in Macau if he hadn't already discovered the Malay Peninsula. Its romance was based on its seedy present and its faintly glorious past.

My grandmother, a (to me) ne'er-do-well if she were a man, was supported mainly by my mother, who married someone fairly well off, that is, my father. He was a good-looking man and a good catch, and his salary supported a family of seven or eight people. I believe at least three of her children were living with my grandmother; they were of school age and my father paid for their tuition and living expenses. My mother told me that she herself was often short of money, because my grandmother was constantly asking her for more. I have never heard that my grandmother ever had a job of any kind; so looking after the teenaged children was her full-time job.

What did she spend her money on? I asked my mom, feeling aggrieved on behalf of my dead father, whose easygoing nature was seemingly being taken advantage of.

Don't know, I never asked. I just thought it was my duty to give her what she wanted if I could.

My mother's answer was deeply dissatisfying to me, someone who values rational behaviour and despises blind obedience. But her attitude also explains her eventual bitterness. Her docility and filial piety, to her, deserved her mother's gratitude and love, neither of which she received. (When I stayed with my grandmother in Hong Kong for two years, my mother had to pay her an allowance monthly, as if my grandmother was a paid nanny.)

Fortunately, I was blithely unaware of these adult miseries during my stay in Macau. I enjoyed visiting my grandmother's house; I enjoyed playing with the children of my parents' friends; I enjoyed the journey to Macau, being "chauffeured" on the tricycle, and eating Macanese food (a mixture of Cantonese and Portuguese cuisine).

Because my parents quarrelled less in Macau, the place somehow was linked, in my childish mind, to familial and marital happiness.

A House in Macau

My grandmother's house was built in an old style of architecture that might still exist in the countryside in Southern China. The street is called Rua do Volong, a transliteration of the Chinese name, which literally means Peace and Prosperity Street. Rua do Volong is a short block west of Rua do Campo, which is a long thoroughfare that turns into Avenida do Conselheiro Ferreira de Almeida. The Chinese call this long avenue Holland Park Road. The Holland Park does not refer to the posh neighbourhood in London. No doubt Dutch settlers lived in this area historically. Not far from Rua do Volong lived Dr. Sun Yat Sen, the father of modern China. My mother remembered his first wife, whom she described as a humble and unpretentious woman who did her own market shopping, unlike Sun's more glamorous wife, one of the Soong sisters. Dr. Sun's house is now a memorial, a lovely quiet spot away from the highrises and traffic.

19 Rua do Volong is the Chinese end of a street of elegant Portuguese colonial apartments. The Portuguese buildings are refurbished in their — presumably — original butter yellow trimmed in red, with the shutters, the railings, and the doors painted green. My grandmother's house had a citrus yellow door. In 2005, it was still standing but in a dilapidated state. A notice was posted on the door about the unsafe condition of the place. In my memory, the front door had a kind of stoop. It opened into a very dark hallway and there was no electric light in that part of the house. In my memory, the inside of the front of the house reminds me of a Dutch painted interior — dark and narrow. Then rooms, and the kitchen at the back, which opened into a courtyard. But it was not a garden; my grandmother kept poultry there. It stank of chicken shit. The floor inside was tile. Cold, which was good for hot tropical days.

If I had embroidered my memories, it is because I felt that the reading public deserves a more interesting (and Portuguese) version of my life. Writing for an audience immediately changes one's focus as one rearranges events, actions and their consequences. To let someone hear one's voice is always an act of seduction. I want to be alluring in my accounts. I want to establish a rapport that will enhance the way I am perceived. Let words have the same function as a perfume or a red lipstick on a woman; let words camouflage and mislead.

It is true that I was born in Macau, but I grew up mainly in Hong Kong. Though I didn't attend school in Macau, I do remember struggling up those wide, sweeping steps in the garden of Santa Rosa Convent School. A picture remains — my mother, dressed in cheongsam, talking to a nun in traditional wimple and habit. A picture of two women of different races, one Chinese, the other Portuguese. My mother was a petite and slender woman in her youth. She would be in her thirties then. Very attractive, with delicate features. She had a good figure, and often wore cheongsam until after my father died and her social status as a tai-tai was diminished. (She could look like a shorter and smaller version of Maggie Cheung's character in *In the Mood for Love*.) In contrast, the nun was dramatically enfolded in voluminous layers of clothes. Shapeless, slightly threatening, with her face largely hidden behind the black headdress. They were standing in the garden, surrounded by palm trees and flowering bushes. I believe they were discussing me. Probably the nun, the principal, was advising my mother which school she should send me to in Hong Kong. Presumably my mother took the advice and I was educated for twelve years by another convent, the Maryknoll Sisters School, in Hong Kong.

So I didn't live with my grandmother in Macau. I did live with her eventually in Hong Kong. But that is another story.

We still had relatives in Macau even after the family moved back to Hong Kong — my mother's aunt and her family, for one. (I was ordered to visit the grave of my grandmother's sister at St. Michael's Cemetery a few years ago. I was given the vaguest of directions and was convinced that I would never find the grave. To my surprise, I stumbled upon it almost immediately.) After our move, I went back to

Macau to visit regularly, whenever I was on holiday. I was interested in the soldiers from Angola and Mozambique. I spent time walking around Macau in the evening, looking at the lights from the shops, looking at people, looking at traffic. Macau, in my memory, is present permanently in connection with a neuroses-free childhood.

Macanese Snapshots

In the 50s, one travelled to Macau by ferry, not dissimilar to the cross-channel ferry from Dover to Ostende. Maybe smaller. Some of the trips when I was very young were overnight crossings, so that we arrived in Macau during the morning. We didn't always stay with my grandmother. I also remember a house that belonged to friends of my parents. Nothing fancy, and certainly demolished now. Were these early journeys the reason why I am perpetually restless? (As soon as I unpack from one trip, I would cast about for the next one, even if it cannot take place until next year.) Students write about the excitement of their summer holidays, but they are equally excited to be home, to begin a new term, to be invited to parties. At a young age, excitement is generalized. But as one accumulates experiences, excitement becomes differentiated. Perhaps I was equally excited about going to Macau at the age of five as I was about going to Christmas midnight mass. But in middle age, I rank the excitement of a journey above all other life experiences.

These friends of my parents had a daughter my age. I thrilled to have some company to play with, since I was an only child. As we grew older — eight? nine? — we spent evenings out with other but older friends. They must be older, since I remember drives, and we couldn't possibly be the drivers. One of our favourite pastimes was to cruise slowly along the corniche of Macau, comprising the Avenida da Republica, Avenida da Praia Grande, and Avenida de Lisboa, which encircles the lovely San Francisco Garden, named after the seminary that was on site and not the American city. The scenery then was far more heartbreakingly beautiful than now.

A long curve of seawall lined by old banyan trees, with locals fishing, or couples necking, or family picnicking around laybys. The benches were favourite resting areas for friends to spend an evening chatting and smoking. The other side of this sweep of road was lined by villas in the Portuguese-Macanese style. Though I didn't know then, one of these villas is the Bela Vista, until 1999 a jewel of a boutique hotel operated by the Mandarin Oriental, now the residence of the Portuguese consul. Rather than admiring the architecture, my girlfriend and I, as well as those teenagers in the car, would whoop and whistle at the lovers, and laugh raucously as the guilty couple sprang apart at the noise and the headlight. (Chinese couples necking in public places always feel guilty —touching intimately in public is such an un-Chinese way to behave.)

While we were not busy frightening perfectly innocent people, we walked around the centre of the peninsula: the Avenida de Almeida Ribeiro, on which is located some gems of Macanese architecture (Leal Senado, the Central Post Office, the 1568 Santa Casa da Miseracórdia, apparently the oldest European charity in China); we sat and watched people in the Largo do Senado and ate sesame candies; we picked over the goods sold in the street stalls on Rua dos Mercadores. I especially remember the bright lights, the yellow gold, and the red price tickets in the windows of the many jewellery stores at the Chinese end of Avenida de Almeida Ribeiro, the arcaded end that debouches into the Rua das Lorchas, the warehouses, the cheap hotels, and the ferry terminal.

During our recherché-trip recently, my mother took me to the famous and truly unique Rua da Felicidade. I don't remember it from my childhood, and no wonder. My mother pointed out the red-lacquer shutters and front doors and told me that they used to be brothels. The houses are two storeys high, with a half-Dutch door. Now, some have been renovated as shops, and some into restaurants. Turn a corner and one looks into Beco da Felicidade, a little lane and courtyard much like what one would find in China, away from Shanghai and Beijing. Only three minutes from the Largo do Senado one walks into a remnant of nineteenth-century China.

Pilgrimages

Yet, on recent visit in the 90s and again in 2005, Macau was not at all a place in genteel decline, ready to become a part of someone's colonial nostalgia. Instead, it has become part of China again. Building construction was everywhere. Population was growing, mainly thanks to the influx of "immigrants" from mainland China. I had not seen the city since the 70s, before I myself immigrated to Canada. But I had very clear and strong memories of the Macau of my past. It is something I cling to, now more than ever. After almost thirty years, I still cannot accept the northern winter of Canada. Yes, it is all about climate, landscape, vegetation. And more. I also knew that I should be prepared for disappointment.

December is a good time to visit Macau, since the average temperature in the winter months was around the mid 20s, and not the stifling mid 30s. Having arranged to leave my luggage at the hotel in Hong Kong, I took a hydrofoil to Macau. The trip took only a bit over an hour. Pretty uneventful, except I was amused at the announcements being made in Cantonese, English, and Portuguese. The ride wasn't unlike the ferry ride between Vancouver and Victoria on the Vancouver Island, except the hydrofoil didn't have decks for the passengers. In a way, the passengers were captives in this moving vessel. We looked out but we couldn't breathe in the sea air.

What one saw immediately, as one neared Macau, were construction cranes everywhere near the Porto Exterior (Outer Harbour). The Portuguese sailors who first approached and settled in Macau hundreds of years ago would have been astonished to find, instead of a sleepy, fishing village, a small city emulating its larger cousin, Hong Kong. In the 90s, one could still see around the harbour towards Baia da Praia Grande. In 2005, the bay has been filled and two artificial lakes were created — Lago Sai Van and Lago Nam Van. Together with a sizeable landfill project, Macau greets its visitors with its insistent modernity. Naturally, compared to Hong Kong, Macau is still somewhat provincial. But one hopes that its provinciality will save it from the aggressive construction–and–destruction programme that characterizes the former British colony.

The Corniche

Unlike in Hong Kong, one can walk around most of Macau's waterfront. Even the newly filled area south of the Porto Exterior, the gridded blocks between Avenida de Amizade and Avenida Dr. Sun Yat Sen was made interesting by the Cultural Centre of Macau and the Art Museum. The museum holding is puny compared to the attempted grandness of the building and plaza, but the whole complex sits elegantly on the shimmering edge of the South China Sea. If one walks quickly westward and averts one's eye from the horrific sight of the Lisboa Hotel/Casino, so ugly in its spectacularly failed Gaudiesqueness, one reaches the old Macau corniche of Praia Grande and Avenida da Republica — old villas looking out to the sea, old banyan trees shading the esplanade, old cobble-stoned walks and benches. At the tip of the peninsula is Barra Hill, where a former seventeenth-century fortress has been converted into a pousada, nestling in the austere stone cliff. (In the early mornings and late evenings, one could almost hear these urban remains of the nineteenth century sigh with sadness.)

One can't really see the water as one walks north towards Rua das Lorchas because of the warehouses at the docks, but further north, where Macau meets China, one can stroll around the Sun Yat Sen Park. The west side of the peninsula is ringed by Avenida da Ponte da Amizade, with streets leading back into the centre of the city. Without a doubt, the picturesque side of the peninsula is the southeast side, the former residents of the colonial officials, now handed over to the Chinese authority, and the resident of the present Portuguese consulate. The combination of the port, the old fortress, the Bishops' Palace, the streets winding along the hillside, the faded elegance of nineteenth-century houses — Macau looks an awful lot like Porto.

Livraria Portuguesa, Rua S. Domingos 18–20

A treasure. A nondescript building in the crowded centre of Macau, surrounded by crumbling colonial Portuguese buildings, some dating back to the 1500s. A stone-throw away from the very attractively tiled Largo do Senado. Across the street from S. Domingos, a buttery-yellow church from the sixteenth century, still much used by Catholic

Macanese. Turn left from the front door of the bookstore — Travessa de S. Domingos. Cozy little Portuguese cafés with fresh pastries. Turn right and up the hill — Monte Forte, the ruins of St. Paul, built by the Jesuits in 1602, the museum.

Inside the bookstore — the best selection of books on Macau in Portuguese and in English. Fado CDs. Prints. Local handmade figurines. Local characters browsing. People greeting each other in Portuguese but the owners are ethnic Chinese. We conversed in Cantonese. English not a useful language.

The Museum of Macau, like the Maritime Museum and the Macau Museum of Art, was built between 1997 and 1999, before the handover. They form a Portuguese cultural legacy, together with the numerous churches, the houses, the tiled street signs, the Eurasian Macanese who continue to live here, to remind visitors and the new Chinese masters alike that Macau has, for better or worse, imbibed Portuguese history and language, which makes this a unique place in East and Southeast Asia.

The museum showcases the predictable Chinese artefacts of the pre-colonial era, as well as those of the colonial encounter. If one wants to see a more "authentic" presentation of colonial life in Macau (as much as any museum exhibits could be an authentic representation of real life), one would do better to visit the Taipa Houses Museum, where complete houses of colonialists are recreated, as if they were still living there. What interested me more in the museum was the exhibition of twentieth-century Macau, with a reading of poetry by Pessoa, who has influenced some Macanese poets in the 20s and 30s. As I picked up the headphone and listened to the various Portuguese readers reciting words I didn't understand, I was transported to some land that was at once my home and a foreign country.

Churches

Many. Their Anglicized names — St. Paul, 1602. Chapel of Our Lady of Guia, 1626. Chapel of Our Lady of Penha, 1622. St. Francis Xavier, 1907, a newcomer. St. James, 1629. St. Michael, 1875. Our Lady of Carmel, 1885. St. Anthony, 1558. St. Lazarus, 1576. The Cathedral, 1576. The Seminary of St. Joseph, 1746 (one of my uncles studied there).

St. Lawrence, 1569. St. Augustine, 1586 (my parents lived near the church, one of their several Macanese addresses). S. Domingos, 1587. By no means an exhaustive list.

Not overly ornate inside, many of these churches are baroque architectural gems. Some have been destroyed and rebuilt. And most wonderful of all, they are used and they are looked after. They are a tourist attraction — the mainland Chinese loved gawking at these architectural artefacts that are a rarity in China. The churches' proximity to each other gives a vivid sense of Macau's Catholic and Portuguese past, more so than the museums or books. On summer days, they are sanctuaries from the heat and noise outside. In winter, they remind the visitors of the world of contemplation, of reflection, of inwardness. The plazas in front become a place of congregation. People sit and eat their snacks. Exchange news. Fan themselves. Watch other people. The churches, though Macau is no longer a Catholic city, create interconnected communities that are lacking in Hong Kong. In that, Macau remains very Portuguese.

Daily Life and Street Scenes

A hot day. No shades on Trevessa de S. Domingos. A steep slope. An old woman, certainly past retirement age, trudged slowly uphill, pushing a cart of folded cardboard boxes. That would be her livelihood — transporting cardboard boxes for small businesses?

Forte Monte. Two Chinese women engaged in sweeping, very leisurely, the dead leaves on the terrace. An unending task, since the terrace was sizeable and the wind kept interfering.

Still Forte Monte. The old ammunition room? Now a little teahouse tucked away as one climbed up to the lookout. Two women, mother and daughter, serving tea, soft drinks, fruits, and smiles. A bonus — frangipani in little vases on the plain wooden tables.

Rua do Almirante Sérgio. A mixture of Portuguese restaurants (I found the business card of O Porto Interior Restaurante in a pile of papers), cave-like seedy shops, pencil-narrow alleys, noisy humanity. Walked into a shop that sold miscellaneous foods and alcohol. Two old men came out of the back, wearing their underwear. It was a hot day, and they were probably having dinner. They pulled on pants and shirts in order to serve the tourists.

Took some pictures of a gorgeous Portuguese apartment building, four storeys high, on Rua de Sé, just before the steps take one down to Avenida de Almeida Rubeiro. Someone — the landlord, the city — has the good sense to renovate the building. It has iron filigree balconies and some decorative flourishes that are influenced by the Manueline architecture. When my mother and I were walking past this building later, she pointed at it and said, *Your father and I lived here.*

Then she told me how a young man, a refugee from Japanese-occupied Southern China, was dying in the doorway and asked her for a drink of water. He thanked her afterwards and shortly died. (What happened to the corpse? I didn't dare ask, as my mother was getting upset.) *Why didn't you save him*, I did ask, ever the naïve Westernized one. *There were so many refugees in those war years. We could only help ourselves*, sighed my mother, who was a very pragmatic woman.

The building held haunting memories for her; it was hauntingly beautiful to me.

Pousada de Sao Tiago

The room has red flagstone floor. The door to the bathroom is a wood sliding door. The furniture has Manueline design. The balcony looks out to a Chinese village, the Porto Interior, and the red tiled rooftops of the lower parts of the pousada. Below walk the tourists who come to visit the ancient St. James chapel.

Because the pousada is part of the former fortress on Barra Hill, its predominant feature is rock. One enters the hotel through a passage tunnelled out of the rock. One walks up stairways with rock faces on both sides. One swims in the swimming pool nesting on top of a rock ledge. The hotel is not very visible from the street because the rock cliffs shelter it.

The pousada advertised breakfast at 7.30. At 7.30 I went down for breakfast. No one in sight. I sat down and admired the glint of morning sun on the water, the distant village that was China, the trees swaying on the terrace, the few boats resting. The music was some 70s Western pop played at the wrong speed. A Chinese waiter, very young, came stumbling out from the back area. He stood politely to take the order from these strange tourists who got up so early. When asked if it was too early for breakfast, he nodded innocently and said, *It's too early*.

Factually, I only spent some summer weeks in Macau, and then only when my father was healthy enough to travel. But, while I would never consider moving back to Hong Kong, I would love to spend part of every year in Macau — to write, to read, to dream, to walk along the waterfront, to sit in S. Domingos or St. Augustine and reflect, to play Fado on a portable player, to watch the sunrise over the Chinese village on the mainland, to even have tea at the very gaudy Lisboa Casino Hotel, or to have Macanese dinner at the Algarve restaurant … It is as if I were born Portuguese culturally, but because of my race, had to be brought up in a Chinese environment, and I have been rebelling ever since. The fact that I spent years at an American convent further divided my cultural loyalty.

Rua do Volong

Doorway of my grandmother's house
on Rua do Volong in 2005

Rua da Felicidade, Macau in 2005. Former brothels

Apartment on Rua de Sé, Macau 2005. My parents
lived there during the Japanese invasion of Hong Kong

Hong Kong

The Dandy and the Gambler

If my father were still alive today, I wouldn't be writing this narrative, nor would I be living in Canada. He would have risen in rank at the bank; I would have followed in the family tradition of going into banking. I might be significantly better off in material terms. But I would not have become an academic.

He was not an authoritarian. He wasn't even a disciplinarian. But in the Chinese tradition, his words were law and I wouldn't have gone against his wishes.

My father came from a landowning family who made money in gold and money exchange in Southern China. Since World War II, the Ng family home — a classic courtyard compound of several houses linked by gardens and interior alleys — had been divided among the sons. By then, my father's share of the house and land consisted of a dilapidated two-storey section with a high wall, a narrow door that could be accessed via a narrow alley, and a roof of broken tiles. I have never been there, but my mother brought back pictures and some kind of land title. The location was about an hour's taxi drive from Guangzhou (Canton City). My father was the only son of the third son of the Ng patriarch. I think the family fortune was in decline already when my father left China for Hong Kong in his youth. I certainly don't remember any talk of family money left to him, though he seemed to have had a pampered childhood. One of the stories that were passed down was that he was kidnapped by bandits as a child for ransom. Another story was that he didn't know how to wash his own feet until quite old because he always had his own maid. Certainly my father never lifted a finger in any kind of housework. I doubted that he had ever gone into the kitchen in any of the places we had lived in. If he wanted tea, the maid, or my mother, or I would bring it to him. I think I even used to run his bath for him.

He spoilt me when I was a child — played with me, allowed me to make noises, tolerated my whims. He was disappointed and embarrassed when I didn't do well in primary school; when my grades picked up and I started to excel in secondary school, he was too ill to care. (But he had a sense of humour. He knew I would do poorly in the city-wide exam that all primary school students had to take to qualify for secondary schools, and joked that if I passed, God must be holding my hands.)

My father was another example of the paradox of Hong Kong Chinese and colonial cultural interchanges. He spoke no English and, though recognizing the political power of the British, he had little fondness or respect for British rule. The fact that he worked for a bank owned by communist China also affected his beliefs a bit, though not enough for him to give up his love of daily pleasures and extravagances. In style, he emulated whatever was elegance. He wore tailored double-breasted suits and tailored traditional Chinese gowns lined in fur. Those were gorgeous clothes in very fine fabrics — cashmere, wool, silk. After he died, my mother asked the tailor to make two fur-lined jackets from the fur of my father's gowns. He wore ascots with polo shirts and baggy pants with pleated waist. He enjoyed Western and Chinese cuisines, as long as they were well prepared. And he took us regularly to Hollywood movies — John Wayne was a favourite, as was Errol Flynn. Among the films we saw as a family, I remember *El Cid, Ben Hur, Cleopatra, The Greatest Show on Earth* ...

For a Chinese man, my father was tallish — 5'7" or 8" and slim. He didn't really look like Tony Leung, but the Hong Kong film star always reminded me of my father, because of his melancholy stillness. I don't think my father was a jolly man, but he enjoyed life so much that he gave the impression of being alert and full of energy. His favourite evening pastime was reading classical Chinese texts, until we bought a television set and he would watch some television.

I don't know how much my father made, but there was enough money to send me to a private school, to eventually buy a car and hire someone to wash it weekly, to buy an apartment in a decent residential neighourhood, to take taxis when we had no car, and to eat out regularly, especially on the weekends.

At the bank, I know that my father would have a quick lunch at some restaurant nearby; then he would take a nap in his office. He was the loans manager of the main branch of the bank when I was in my early teens. He often socialized with clients — posh dinners or even nightclubs. Sometimes he would take me with him to the dinners. Once

I saw a client pass him some money during the meal. I suppose that partly augmented our lifestyle. Another way the family income was augmented was through his gambling.

My father did not play mahjong merely as a pastime. He kept meticulous records of his wins and losses in a little book. After a big win, I might get new clothes, or we would take a trip to Macau, or just have an extravagant dinner out, depending on the amount. He also lost, and those losses were the main reason that my parents fought. In my childish eyes and in my memories, these were acrimonious fights. Shouting matches, mainly with my mother shouting and my father grumbling defensively. Tears. Doors banging. Cancelled outings because my mother would be sulking. The main difference between my father and mother was that, while my father took adversities stoically, my mother indulged in dramatic responses, from verbal abuse to prolonged sullenness to bed-riddenness. I thought those scenes were terrifying when I was a child, and disappointing when I was older, because the rare occasion when the three of us could play happy family was ruined. I sometimes would suggest to my father that we should go out — just the two of us — an early sign of disloyalty to my mother. Did he agree, or did he stay home loyally by his sullen wife? These scenes were one of the various causes that led to my critical resentment of my mother's personality.

Arguably, my father was the culprit, since he was acting irresponsibly with the money that supported the family. But I learned early that it wasn't acting responsibly that was endearing; doing the right thing without a sense of humour and without sensitivity could evoke an equally negative response. My mother was a perpetual wet blanket, putting a damper on the potential fun my father and I could have. It doesn't take a family therapist to disentangle the family dynamics of the Ng household. The father — already the authority figure based on cultural tradition, also was a soft-spoken, impulsive, pleasure-loving person who never indulged in violent words or action. The mother — a nervous woman who wanted to maintain her control on the household and on the upbringing of her only daughter; who often invested trivial matters with the importance of ethical issues; who, because she was not articulate, expressed her anger and frustration through verbal abuse and sometimes, physical abuse. At ten or twelve or even fourteen, I didn't have the kind of insight necessary to understand my mother. I only knew that when she was nearby, life was more complicated, more stressful, and sometimes, more painful. That psychological memory remains with me to this day.

(As an adult, I often reminded my mother that she was making my father miserable with her constant bickering and hysterics, and that that was my most vivid childhood memory. Her defence was that they were a loving couple, regardless of the many fights. It was probably true, in that my father was an indulgent husband — but his weakness was that he never tried to discuss matters with my mother. He ignored her when she was "acting up" or humoured her, waiting for her temperamental outbursts to dissipate. Not a good pedagogical approach.)

Even my father's gambling was fascinating to me. He took chances. He was obsessive. He was brilliant — he didn't need to look at the mahjong counters because his fingertips could tell all the different designs. He was a sought-after partner in high-stake games. The unpredictability of gains and losses meant that there were weeks when we had to be frugal but also days when we lived like toffs. I inherited some of his traits — the impulsiveness, the obsessiveness, the love for elegance and style; but also his recklessness with money, and his ability to disappoint while promising so much. (Most likely reason for his not showing up on weekends to pick me up from my grandmother's place — a gambling event.)

I also was influenced by the image of an adult who could sit still for hours reading, with a cup of tea at his elbow. It was an unusual image in Hong Kong, a city where people spent, and still do, all their energy in doing things — running across the road, impatiently tapping on the elevator call button, talking fast and eating, jumping off busses and rushing to catch the ferry — and most important of all, making money. My father had a cavalier attitude towards money, no doubt a residual attitude from his family background and childhood upbringing. (Another story told about dad — his first job as an apprentice with a gold merchant was to sweep the floor, which he did badly.)

Without English, my father would have been reduced to a state of dependency if he had come to Canada. What could he do? Open a corner grocery store? My father, who had never lifted his finger in any labour, stocking shelves with tins and packages of cereal. He would have hated it. (We don't often understand why Asian immigrant men could be silently hostile, as grocery store clerk, as taxi driver, as waiter — being a hapless immigrant who has to take menial jobs in a foreign culture could be a psychologically debilitating experience, especially when he is a person of some social prestige and power in his home country.) I would have hated to have to witness my father being emasculated by Western culture, unprotected by his unassailable social position as the pater familia and the breadwinner and the bank manager, surrounded by his circle of friends and colleagues in Hong Kong.

My father died when I was sixteen, and one of the last things he said to my mother and me was that now, we could freely leave Hong Kong without him.

My father died when I was beginning to be a difficult teenager, so he didn't have to deal with my rebelliousness. All his energy in his last months was spent in hoping in vain that his cancer would be treatable; in denying that his weight had gone down below 100 lbs; in swallowing and digesting food while every mouthful caused excruciating pain. (I wince now when I read how Freud had to have a jaw prosthesis fitted after his operation — that would be extremely painful.) Towards the end of his life, I was tired of being a nurse, changing his pyjamas and bed sheets constantly, fetching whatever he wanted for him, tiptoeing around the apartment, not having fun, not being allowed to have any time to myself. I also failed miserably in any attempts to comfort him — I knew he was dying and thought it was hypocritical to lie about it. While everyone else was busy concocting some kind of fairytale diagnosis, I kept silent. So his death, predicted and inevitable, came as a relief to me.

Since my father died when I was still a teenager, I have only wonderful memories of him. This part of my narrative would have been quite different if he had lived to a ripe old age.

After his death, I moved into my parents' bedroom and slept on his single bed — in retrospect it was kind of macabre. But my mother wanted me to keep her company. After his death, I indulged in hobbies that my father would have frowned upon. I watched the English-language television channel exclusively, telling my mother that I needed to practise my English. Thus I followed series such as *Peyton Place, Somerset Maugham Hour, Bonanza, The Six Wives of Henry VIII* … I became an avid fan of Western pop music, buying records by James Taylor, Joni Mitchell, The Beatles and so on. I lunched out, when I was allowed to, with friends at Wimpy Bar. (I think one can still find some of this burger franchise in England. My first Wimpy burger in England was in Wembley, a totally miserable suburb.) I wore mini-skirts. And I took German courses at the Goethe Institute. My mother, being unschooled, thought all learning was beneficial. My father would have objected — what good would knowing German do for my career as a high-flying financial manager?

But I was freed by his death.

Highrises and Apartments

We didn't travel much except to Macau, but we moved houses a lot. I remember clearly five different apartments we lived in, until my parents bought a flat in Causeway Bay Road and we settled down. In 1973, my mother sold the flat to finance our move to Canada. But this peripatetic childhood must have given me a taste for travelling. Since the late 70s, I have been going to Europe nearly every year. After moving to Alberta from Vancouver, I have flown back and forth averaging nine times a year. And since I am an academic and not some business executive who has work-related travels, this is an indication of profound restlessness. Even though I should be used to travelling by now, I still plan every trip — no matter how short — as if I were moving house, down to every last detail. There is a great fear of being too grounded, but also a great fear of being homeless. (A friend told me once that he was amused at my habit of carrying my passport with me daily. I stopped doing that recently.)

The first flat we lived in as a family of three was leased. It was in a four-storey walk-up, long since demolished. The living room was the room facing Electricity Road in Causeway Bay, a neighbourhood that we seemed to favour. The floor was tiled. At least, part of it must have been. The kitchen and washroom were at the back. I don't think we had a bathtub or shower stall, so we must have washed in a big wooden tub. (That was in the early 50s; not all flats had running water and shower.) We had a maid — she was an old woman — to my childish eyes at least. Compliant and ineffectual — that is how I remember her. I wasn't a considerate child, in that I took advantage of the little power I had over another person, based on socio-economic facts, and often ordered her around. I also remember pummelling her with my little fists when I got bored with her stories. It was not an endearing gesture, but one that indicated impatience and an egotism that, luckily, was eventually tempered by education and life experiences.

My childhood was quite idyllic. By all accounts, I was a happy and chatty child, loved games and laughed a lot. Not a particularly thoughtful child. I was well brought up, and that, ironically, was my downfall.

We had a telephone in an alcove along the dark narrow hallway, quite near the front door. I must have been six, certainly finished with kindergarten. (One fond memory I have of early school days is of my father taking me to kindergarten, a few blocks from the flat. He carried me over his shoulders. A rare occurrence, since physical exertions were unusual with my father.) One day the phone rang and I answered. I only know that I had a long conversation with some "stranger" who asked me all kinds of questions regarding my parents, to which I obligingly supplied the answers, because I was taught to respect adults. Obviously my parents were not around and the maid was out shopping at the market, or even gone for good by then. But melodramatically, my problem-free childhood — father taking me to school, a maid, a benign mother, a cool dark flat all to our own — came to end, and to this day, I believe it was because of that phone call.

Who was the caller? No one ever told me. I heard vague accusations that it was someone from my father's place of work, spying on him. (My father worked all his adult life, after I was born, for a communist bank owned by China. Employees were supposed to be staunch communists, much as the Vatican would expect its employees to be fervent Catholics.) Apparently, I even asked the caller if he (or was it a she?) had all the information he (or she) wanted. But whoever it was, the effect of my lengthy, revealing conversation was that there were almighty rows between my parents, and my parents separated, and I got unloaded onto my grandmother, who at this time had moved from Macau with her several adult children to North Point, Hong Kong. (I learned later that my mother paid my grandmother a monthly fee. It came about that my mother thought I wasn't getting the food that she had paid for. In effect, my mother suspected that my grandmother was cheating her own daughter over her granddaughter. I believe my mother.)

My parents and I never discussed this event again, the same way we tried to avoid discussing any major issues concerning us. And I never asked my mother — I am afraid of what I might find out. Hong Kong is also the kind of city that encourages one not to delve too much — into situations, into people's backgrounds, into one's psyche. The excessive population, the excessive traffic, the excessive dramas of daily life — any mysteries should be left as such. The culture of finding out the truth regardless of the cost (the Western ideal), or the culture of exposing secrets for the purpose of selling news (the Western media) is an acquired practice in Hong Kong. Hong Kong media share with their Western counterparts the love of trivial information. But Chinese also respect authority and power. Wealthy people have power. The government has authority and power. Hong Kong people enjoy knowing secrets; they also can live without this knowledge. And for those who have to live without power and wealth, the ways to deal with unpleasantness is to ignore it or bury it. (The ostrich approach to life even infects my attitude towards something as marginal as watching sports. I cannot witness a tense contest involving athletes or teams I support. During World Cup 2006, I had to regularly leave the place where the match was being broadcast in Berlin when either Italy or Portugal was playing.

Nor have I yet seen Roger Federer win a Wimbledon final, because the fear of an undesirable outcome outweighs the desire to watch.)

My grandmother lived with three sons and a daughter — all grown up — in one big room. A kind of open-plan living! The flat was part of government-subsidized housing, similar to the council flats in England — long corridors of undifferentiated doors, rows of corridors one on top of another, concrete boxes leaning on each other. Dead social space. The housing complex — ironically called Healthy Village (Chinese have no sense of irony, only infinite optimism, when they name places, people, businesses) — was horrible, though I must have managed somehow. Living in such congested conditions, both inside the flat and in the housing complex, gave me a life-long abhorrence of proximity to people and of enclosed space. Crowded buses, crowded cinemas, crowded planes, and so on. I didn't stay long there — only as long as it took my parents to sort out their various affairs (sexual?) and problems (financial?) — but it seemed, and still seems, an eternity. Two years were an eternity to a child.

Most happy and unhappy memories from those years of exile: waiting for my father to pick me up on the weekend. He would take me to a restaurant in North Point called Venice. We ordered a set meal of three courses — a soup, a main dish (usually cod fillet with cream sauce or mixed grill), a dessert. I visited the bachelor room that he rented from a family from Shanghai on Temple Road, at that time a fairly respectable middle-classed neighbourhood. Stayed overnight and played with the children of his landlady. He took me back on Sunday to the concrete jungle. Compared to Healthy Village, private apartment blocks on Temple Road were posh. There were courtyards, trees, Mercedes and chauffeurs, maids who gossiped in the backyard, an old-fashioned elevator with brass fittings, and wood parquet floor. Outside of the window of my father's room was the hillside where houseless people — usually refugees from China — set up illegal shacks.

But when he didn't come, for whatever adult reason, it was tragic. I would sit outside the front door on a stool and wait. By evening, it was obvious that he couldn't make it that weekend. I bawled and bawled, and my rather unsympathetic grandmother, not the most sensitive person I have known, would with indifference tell me to get over it. (I should be fair — she had seven children and was widowed at a relatively young age. Being illiterate and not trained to do anything, her life seemed a constant struggle to stay afloat of bills. My father paid for many of the bills since he married my mother; then the children grew up and found decent jobs. But wariness and a kind of *Mother Courage* pragmatism dominated her life attitude.)

I feared my grandmother because all her children revered her, and I was told always to obey her. I did to the best of my ability, but it didn't stop me developing a dislike for her, which lasted till she died. Contributing to my antipathy would be her use of corporal punishment and telling my aunt or uncle that I had misbehaved during the day, so that I would get another dose of scolding from her children. I could see that she loved her youngest daughter more than my mother, the eldest and for years, the bill-payer, whom she treated with perfunctory attention.

In those years, I had no idea, and still have no idea, where my mother lived. She was truly lost to me — I didn't even have a telephone number; but somehow, I don't remember feeling forlorn because of her absence as I did my father's. I also sensed, without the critical knowledge I do now, that my grandmother represented all that was questionable, even despicable, in a woman brought up in traditional Chinese culture — greediness, ignorance that was allowed to become so ingrained that it came across as wisdom, superstition, and a repulsive pragmatism based on a hard life. "My life was such a struggle, bringing up seven children through the war, I have no time for others' misfortune" — that could be my grandmother's mantra. Nothing illogical with that attitude — but an attitude that could not be called endearing.

Eventually, my parents moved back together. The three of us lived in my father's bachelor rented room. I didn't understand why there should be a dip in our family fortune, since my father wasn't unemployed — he still had the same job at the bank as far as I knew. Was it inflation in the late 50s? Housing shortage? Gambling debts? Whatever the cause, we crammed ourselves into this one room, and shared a bathroom and kitchen with another family. The flat was quite large, so that the landlord's children — two girls and one boy — had their own room, and the two servants, whom my mother was allowed to use for light chores, had their sleeping quarters near the kitchen. The landlord was from Shanghai, a good-looking refined man, soft-spoken and seemed not to know who I was most of the time. His wife was from Ningpo, a much rougher person, and much more calculating, according to my mother, who had a tense relationship with her. I enjoyed our stay there because, for the first time, I had playmates all the time, though the two girls, very similar in age to me, were snobbish enough to remind me that my parents were only renting a room from them. This hostility became most apparent when we fought over our respective schools. I went to Maryknoll Sisters School and they went to St. Paul's Convent. They thought St. Paul's was a better school with smarter and wealthier students. I was always very humiliated by these jibes but learned to laugh them off as if I didn't care.

Where to live continued to be a problem, especially as I got older and needed my own room. The bank was building an apartment as employee dormitory but it wasn't ready, so we moved temporarily into a more bizarre rental arrangement that could only happen in places where living space was at a premium. We rented two rooms on the second floor in a highrise above a piano business. The two rooms formed part of its storage in a large space it owned but were standing empty. I could play with any of the pianos stored outside of our sub-apartment and for a while, I took piano lessons. It was in that flat that I taught my father how to sign his name in English. I was attending the last year of primary school.

The only time we lived across the harbour on Kowloon side was when we moved into the dormitory apartment. Again, two rooms, with a small living area, and no view to speak of. But it was on the edge of a very posh residential neighbourhood and in the summer evenings, my father would drive us in the second-hand Simca he bought, the first car in the family since I was born, to Kowloon Tong Park for walks. Those evenings were wonderful, because we didn't fight, the three of us; my father was getting a promotion; my mother was feeling relatively healthy; the rent was low; and my father's cancer was in remission. All good things. But the flat was in an ultra ugly building, which my cousin told me in 2005 was still standing, and it was linked in my mind with the rioting in 1967, when pro-China and anti-US demonstrations were quelled by police and SWAT teams arrested protestors in numbers. One day, the special force (I presume) came searching every flat in our building because the apartment was funded by China and housed people working for communist institutions. My father was still at work, but my mother's fifth brother was visiting. He got arrested and was kept overnight in detention. When I recently mentioned this incident to my mother, she denied it ever happened, even though I reminded her that my father thought it was a good joke, in a rather callous way.

My father's last home was back to Causeway Bay. Bayview Mansion, a rather grandiose name given to an ordinary highrise complex, was brand new when we bought our flat. Wood floor, three rooms, plus a large living area, and a bathroom with bathtub and an entirely tiled kitchen. We thought it was the height of luxury based on what we could afford. It was no longer rental living. We were establishing ourselves solidly in the lower-middle class; though we sold the Simca, we travelled by hired cars. My father was not well enough to drive, though he could still go to the bank daily. We weren't poor, but we didn't have the many accessories of my wealthy mates — maids, chauffeur-driven Rolls, designer clothes, and so on. Having our own flat was a start. And we ate out a lot. Certainly we were living in more comfortable conditions than many people in Hong Kong. Once I brought a man I was dating home and he was more than impressed with the size of the apartment and the way it was furnished and the location. He said he felt like a prince sitting on the sofa eating grapes that my mother provided. My mother thought him vulgar.

When I walked through Bayview Mansion again in 2005, I couldn't believe that over thirty years ago, we thought we were living in a nice building. The outside of the highrise was dark with years of dirt; the ground-floor business spaces were occupied by dingy and rather dubious shops. Once the gates were manned by Sikh security guards who proudly stood with rifles on their shoulders. Now, anyone could walk through. The floor in the public areas was unwashed; the lighting too dim for the long corridors. The building looked quite suitable as stage setting for a film about the apocalyptical end of a city — *Children of Men*, for example. Even the location — opposite Victoria Park and adjacent to St. Paul's Convent School — was degraded by more highrises that took over the wide boulevard along the school and the open spaces in front of the south side of the park.

My Colonial Education

Unlike other ethnic writers growing up under colonialism and discovering the freedom of postcolonial identities, I loved my colonial education.

The school I went to summed up the cultural complexity of Hong Kong in the 50s and 60s. From the age of six I started learning, and eventually speaking, English at Maryknoll Sisters School six days a week, while at home it was always Cantonese, since my parents didn't know English. It wasn't, and still isn't, an anomaly for Chinese parents to want to enrol their children in a school run by some Western religious orders, be it Catholic or Protestant. These institutions are considered to be better organized, better staffed, and generally, they do have a reputation that travels well. Two examples will illustrate my point. At the Modern Language Association annual conference one year, I met up with a famous scholar from Hong Kong and we exchanged greetings. Then we exchanged school information, and I felt quite proud that I could mention Maryknoll Sisters School as my alma mater. The other example: Only recently, I was waiting at a specialist office in Vancouver while my mother was getting a gastroscopy. The specialist, being an ethnic Chinese, attracted a predominantly Chinese clientele. I overheard two people discussing the respective merits of two well known boys' schools in Hong Kong, both run by Catholic orders.

The basic assumption is: these schools teach English properly, and proficiency in English translates into career mobility and opportunities.

Actually, that wasn't true in the 60s and still not true today. Certainly at Maryknoll, we studied mainly Western curriculum and the teachers taught in English, except for Chinese Literature and History. But, except for the American nuns, the teachers were Chinese who spoke English with a Chinese accent. Which meant that the students would have to be able to recognize what accent to imitate — a New York accent? A Southern Chinese accent? Or in my case, a British accent? Furthermore, my fellow students didn't really feel comfortable speaking English to each other, though the practice was encouraged. If a student didn't speak in class, as was and still is often the case with Chinese students, and didn't speak English during recess, and didn't speak English at all at home, then she wasn't going to be fluent in English, no matter how good the teachers were.

I actually quite liked speaking out in school, especially in English Literature and Biblical Study classes. And unlike my good friends who avoided speaking English if at all possible, I spoke English mixed with Chinese during recess and lunchtime. My first group of friends in secondary school came from solid Chinese backgrounds — their parents might have had some education, but were from the lower-middle class and spoke no English. Somehow, in my senior years, I drifted away from them and got to spend more time with an elite group of Chinese girls. They came from fairly wealthy backgrounds, with relatives who lived in the U.S.; their parents knew some English; and these girls planned on going to MIT, or Harvard, or UC Berkeley. My parents were not in this Western-educated social class, but I was accepted in this group because my English was considered idiomatic and somehow I managed to mimic a British accent. I learned early in life that linguistic abilities could be a social asset. I also became a teacher's pet because of my ability to converse.

One of the most astonishing teachers I had, not counting the nuns, was a Chinese woman who had just come back from finishing school in Switzerland. She probably came from an ethnically mixed background. She had porcelain skin, wore Chanel suits, and was dropped off each morning by a chauffeur-driven Mercedes. She taught English Literature and, to this day, I still remember that *Little Women* and *Jane*

Eyre were on the course list. One day she asked me to read a few pages from *Little Women* out loud in class (the usual ploy a teacher uses when she wants to lecture less) and afterwards, she said, to herself as much as to the class, that I read beautifully. Of course I cannot tell if that was the beginning of my attachment to literature; but it was a very strong kind of encouragement to an impressionable girl. She also showed me that a woman could be a professional and still have a strong sense of fashion style. We were awestruck by her wealth, her wardrobe, and her English. She also taught French, which all the non-Chinese or Eurasian students took instead of Chinese. I was quite envious of these students, not only because they belonged to the "special" class of expatriates, but also because they could learn French instead of the — to me — dreary history of the many Chinese dynasties and the almost impenetrable classical Chinese texts.

Maryknoll adopted a fairly conventional Western curriculum: English Literature, English Grammar, History, Biology, Chemistry, Mathematics, Music, Physical Education, etc . I was terrible in PE, and was no better in Home Economics. To me, it was entirely irrelevant to learn to make an omelette or to prepare a filet mignon, bake a gateau, clean the kitchen countertop and stove, when at home we only ate Chinese dishes and had a semi-traditional Chinese kitchen walled in tiles, equipped with gas cookers, wok, and steamers. No oven. I supposed this course helped me feel somewhat comfortable when I started eating mainly Western dishes in Canada. At least, I was taught how to hold a fork and a knife, which my mother found awkward to handle. O yes, the course also taught us the difference between a fish and a dessert knife.

(I am exaggerating the gulf between what I learned about eating at home and at school. Ironically, my parents were fans of Western cuisine of a sort. They liked going to restaurants that served fish filet in a cream sauce, or calf liver with fried onion. Wang Kar-wai's *In the Mood for Love* has a wonderful scene in which Tony Leung and Maggie Cheung share a Western meal. That was the kind of place my parents took me to. My mother also liked cooking borscht soup, pork chops, and pomme frites as a special treat. We would eat the meal off Royal

Doulton bone china and use silver-plated cutlery. But these were rare occasions; maybe once a year at most.)

As for physical education, we had to play basketball and volleyball, run, do gymnastics, and other various assorted contortions involving bodily pain. I despised these activities thoroughly, and counting on my good grades in other areas, more or less resigned myself to fail in this course. For some reason, the PE teacher took pity on me, and though I ran with the basketball under my arm as if I were playing rugby, and never even managed to return a weak volley across the net, she passed me.

While the nuns taught me Biblical Study, English Language and Literature (except for that one year when the woman from the Swiss finishing school took over), Chemistry, and in some years, Music, Chinese women teachers were in charge of Civic Science, History, Mathematics, while two Chinese men, whom I thought of as eunuchs in this very woman-dominated milieu, taught Chinese History and Literature. Whether it was a dress code or not, the Chinese women wore cheongsam, the fitted and tailored dress made so glamorous by Maggie Cheung in *In the Mood for Love*, and the men wore suits. Thus were the staff and students at Maryknoll defined by their costumes.

If the nuns were dressed as the brides of Christ, in flowing white robes and a headdress (wimple) of black, the Maryknoll girls were "brides-of-Christ" manqué. In winter we wore a heavy navy wool dress with white Peter-Pan collar and a blue bow tie, and in summer a white variation. No heels. Only black or white Mary Janes. Regardless of cultural and religious backgrounds, we all wore the same uniform that defined us as different not only from those who could not attend a private girl school, but also those who attended "other" private girl schools. While the philosophy behind the uniform partly endorsed the equality of all Maryknoll girls and curbed any signs of personal vanity, ironically the uniform also provided us with a reason to practise pride. We were proud of our Maryknoll uniform and we showed off on the Hong Kong streets and looked down on girls wearing less distinguished school outfits.

But, along with Vatican II the dress code relaxed. The nuns, except for a few very old ones, changed to the modern habit of a blouse and light skirt; the Chinese women teachers, though under no obligations to change, began to wear pantsuits; and instead of the white cotton uniform with Peter Pan collar and tie, we could wear a yellow or a blue pinafore dress. In retrospect, I much preferred the older habits for both nuns and students. We looked like serious business then. The variety of colours, even when confined to white, yellow, and light blue, implied frivolity, after years of living in black and white.

I didn't read Latin or Greek; I didn't learn anything about philosophy or classical civilization. But I received, nonetheless, a solid Western education that prepared me well for university study. And in the 60s, none of us felt that it was bizarre that we should start our mornings with hymn singing, use words such as tuck shop and recess, or to recite poems by Wordsworth or Tennyson on summer afternoons. We sang "Flow Gently Sweet Afton" and "Where the Bee Sucks" in citywide competitions, coached by a woman we thought was somewhat demented, so exaggerated were her gestures and instructions. She also wore a horrible wig that threatened to fall off her head with her vigorous body shaking and arm waving. We never won any singing competition and it wasn't only because I always sang out of tune. In addition to Western classics and twee British folk tunes, we celebrated Christmas, which was normal for me as a Catholic anyway, and we got a day off on July Fourth, because of the American background of the Maryknoll order.

Overall, Maryknoll Sisters School reinforced what I, as a teenager, thought was positive in the colonial culture in Hong Kong. Its very location on the hill affirmed, geographically and symbolically, the superiority of Western culture. The assurance and restrained arrogance of some of the nuns in dealing with the world outside the school, as well as their comfortable lifestyle, confirmed that Westerners did have privileges that Chinese, unless wealthy, did not have. The respect acquaintances accorded the school and my education also reassured me that to be tutored by Westerners was superior to being taught by Chinese. Of course, the nuns belonged to a religious order, and an American one, and were not affiliated with the British colonial power. But to a politically unsophisticated teenager, they were all non-Chinese; they were powerful either intellectually or politically; and I wanted to emulate them.

Growing up in this woman-dominated regime in which men were marginalized also fostered in me the courage to resist the patriarchal doctrine of Confucianist tradition. Even my Catholic parents believed in a world led by men, a family headed by men, a society in which successes were achieved by men. Women's roles were confined to the traditional wife, mother, and filial daughter. But at school, my teachers were professional women. The nuns were powerful within school politics. Of course the Catholic Church was patriarchal as well. But since I never saw the Pope and the priest only came on Wednesday and Saturday to conduct morning mass, I saw the nuns as role models. The Chinese male teachers were not only marginal in numbers. They were also terrible teachers, compared to the women. Again, masculine superiority was not in evidence for the many years I attended Maryknoll.

Those were wonderful days. Summer afternoons spent reading Dickens or Hardy on the school lawn. Nodding off during Chinese classical literature while waiting for the bell to ring for recess. The noise in the tuck shop. The quiet of the chapel. The polished linoleum floor of the corridors. The excitement of changing from summer to winter uniform. The burnt cake in Home Economics. The giggles behind the giant potted palms in the foyer. The view of the hillside from the window of the library. I loved school.

Of course, my affection stemmed from the very difference between Maryknoll and my Chinese cultural background. At school, I could speak in class and was rewarded for it. At home, being the most junior person of the extended family, I had no voice at all. At school, I was with friends with whom I shared ideas, however subversive they might be. At home, I had not much to say to my parents, who were really traditional Chinese who believed in parental authority and in reticence, a Chinese virtue. At school, I was learning and growing intellectually. At home, I was treated as a subordinate and every act of autonomy required a shouting match and hysterical outbursts from my mother and me, while my father escaped behind his newspaper or book.

Like all over-disciplined children, I feared adults in general and especially the adults who had power over me. Every mistake or misdeed promised punishment. If lucky, verbal. If unlucky, corporal. Always psychological, through angry silence and an atmosphere of disapprobation. So my experience with the principal when I was in secondary school over a broken pot was a revelation. A group of us were fooling around during lunch break. I was pushed and to steady my fall, I grabbed the palm fronds of a big pot as I was trundling down the stone steps that led to a sloping lawn. Unfortunately, the pot fell too and broke into pieces. It was a large decorative item and everyone was stunned into silence. While some suggested that we should just leave the scene immediately, I decided that I had better confess to the principal, Sister Stella Marie. (Well, the gardener saw us and though he said nothing, he wasn't going to lie for us. I had no choice.)

The interview was in her office. Sister S.M. was a tall and very clean-looking person. Clear skin, clear eyes, no wisp of hair escaped from under her wimple, though she did have a slight moustache. She listened to me without looking angry. She asked a few questions. Then she asked me to show her where the accident happened. Then she patted me on my shoulder and said that my honesty mitigated the damage in every way. There was no recrimination, but a smile of encouragement. I learned several life lessons from this incident. I was braver than my schoolmates. Sister S.M. was more reasonable than my mother would ever be. A mistake was not always punishable. The more time I spent at school, the less fond I became of my family life. As a matter of fact, because the convent education liberated me, I wanted to become a nun at one point, so thankful was I towards Maryknoll and the Catholic Church. I don't think I had the vocation. The wish was more based on misplaced gratitude.

My education did a lot for me. Even though I came to Canada with functional but less than fluent English, the foundation and training were there. In less than a few months, I managed to reproduce a perfect mimic of Canadian English while retaining a faint British accent. And while I still wrote with dangling modifiers and incomplete sentences in my first year at university, the grammar I learned at Maryknoll helped me overcome any written inadequacies fairly quickly. Having spent years observing Western cultural behaviour, I felt comfortable with my mainly Canadian circle of friends, unlike my relatives, who remained within a predominantly Chinese enclave.

Quick acculturations have their drawbacks, though. I felt less and less attached to my Chinese root. I failed to find a way to bridge the already existing cultural divide between my mother and myself. How ironical it was then, when I studied Postcolonial Theory and found out that I should be critical of my colonial past! The very past that had equipped me to deal with the myriad difficulties involved in transplanting myself in a new culture, to adopt new practices, and to forge a career based absolutely on different demands and standards than those of Chinese Hong Kong. These confusing and conflicting scenarios were not much dealt with theoretically, but I am sure they exist for many who grew up in a colonial culture and have to navigate between shifting loyalties and opposing daily practices. Do I cook in the Chinese way or bake? Should I perm my hair (or even colour it!) or leave it black and straight? More importantly, should I maintain my individualism, be a feminist and refuse to follow any of the conventions expected of a Chinese woman, or should I be the filial and obedient daughter, although my mother and I cannot agree on anything?

Interestingly, my Maryknoll education continues to help me negotiate my life as a Hong Kong Chinese with a British-American education who now lives in Canada and works within the North American academic system. In Biblical Study, we were taught exegesis. We learned to interpret words; we learned to explicate; we were trained to be mentally flexible. That was the only way one could understand the many paradoxes in the New Testament. I see my life as a paradox. It is not a mathematical equation. Logic cannot be applied. Every day I examine my life as if it were a text to be explicated. Each cultural confrontation is analyzed and interpreted as an illustration of the inevitable script of the transnational moment. I am sure that Sister Bernadette never thought that her teaching would have such far-flung influence.

The Nuns versus the Mother

In *Through the Narrow Gate*, Karen Armstrong makes a very strong case that the process of becoming a nun is extremely demanding, and her portrayal of the religious life in a convent is physically and psychologically harrowing. I only saw the Maryknoll Sisters' life from the outside, in that no one other than the nuns and some servants were allowed to penetrate their private quarters. But though I remember that some of the sisters seemed unhappy at times, the ones I knew functioned well in the environment of the convent and school. They became my role models.

If colonialism emasculates native patriarchy, then a convent education undermines maternal authority. At home, I had my grandmother, for a very short period, and, of course, my mother as role models. At school, I looked to a convent of American nuns and assorted qualified teachers to show me what being female could achieve and to illustrate the possibilities of a different life from that of a dependent woman. Therefore, it was ironic that my mother, who wanted so much to have total control over my life, was also the person who "helped" me achieve an independent mind, and eventually, after a long and struggling process, an independent life. Without a doubt, my education in Hong Kong has made me the worst possible sort of daughter for my mother.

Before I begin what some would consider a critical and unfilial portrait of my mother (and by implication, my grandmother, since she was my mother's role model), I should stress that they were products of a patriarchal and stifling tradition that didn't allow women much opportunity to develop their potentials. Anyone who has read Denise Chong's *The Concubine's Children*, or Chen Ying's *Ingratitude*, would get a sense of the narrow intellectual world that Chinese women grew up in at the turn of the century and even in modern China. A woman was expected to be first, a dutiful daughter, then a good wife, and once she became a mother, a dedicated mother. Women internalized the concept that they owed their happiness and well-being to their families and to the men in their lives (fathers, husbands, sons). However, so much subjugation often resulted in the women's need to exert power over someone else. Could be servants; could be poor relatives and stepchildren; or even daughters, especially in a culture that valued sons. In North America, people might go to therapy for all kinds of reasons — shocked by violence witnessed on the street; trauma caused by the death of someone close; depression induced by loss of money or work and so on. Chinese women who spent their lives honouring their fathers, even abusive ones; or serving their husbands, even those who had concubines; or remaining steadfast to their dead husbands' names — they should have had therapy as well. But a whole nation of Chinese women, even those in diaspora, maintain these beliefs because they were traditions.

(Both my grandmother and mother were widowed at a relatively young age — my grandmother in her thirties and my mother in her forties — neither would consider "dating" another man, and neither had considered remarrying. My mother's mantra was that she was a "person of the Ng family and would die a person of the family" when I had hinted, because my Western friends made the suggestions, that she should consider starting a new life with another partner. While it followed the Confucianist concept of womanly virtue, it made life hard for me as the only person who could fulfil her emotional and possible financial needs.) Neither my grandmother nor my mother could be considered unusual cases.

I was the unusual case as a Chinese daughter.

My grandmother was not a loving mother as far as my mother was concerned, and my mother's resentment was very much part of my experience of mother/daughter relationship. But, even though I was constantly in emotional conflict and psychological warfare with my mother, I didn't try to recruit my grandmother as an ally. I ultimately mistrusted them both as possible models for womanhood. Both received very little formal education and had difficulty analyzing problems. Both were dependent on their husbands or their children. Although my mother felt repressed hostility towards her own mother, she obviously followed social instructions that she received as a child and felt that fulfilling family obligations was the priority in her life. After all, what other route could she follow?

With a brood of younger brothers and sisters and a mother who had no employable skills, my mother became effectively the one responsible for rent money, grocery bills, and tuition fees. She achieved this by marrying my father. She was eighteen and judging by the photographs, a very beautiful woman. The insecurity and fears of poverty she experienced stayed with my mother — the desire for social standing and respect; the constant gauging of others' opinions regarding herself; the need for material comforts. When my father was alive, he was supposed to provide her with these needs. After his death, I was expected to take over.

Rationale, self-analysis, and reflection can help a person examine her motives, her failures, her strengths, and help her change in order to transit to a happier state of mind and/or a more productive way of living. This my mother never achieved. Except for minor adaptations, she existed much the same way she was brought up within a Chinese culture that was traditionalist in that it abided by a popularized Confucianist philosophy (although my mother wouldn't recognize it as such), and misogynist in that this culture never valued women enough to believe that education for girls was as essential as for boys. This situation, which was common to the majority of Chinese families, was, in our case, complicated by the influence of Western culture through colonization.

Thus, my mother was a staunch believer in the fixed roles of man and woman in the family. The man provides, and provides well, while the woman rules the domestic arena. My mother also internalized, as all Chinese do, the unassailable nature of filial piety and the rightful expectations of parents. Her hostile feelings towards her mother must have caused her great unhappiness. As if all these dictates were not enough psychological weight, she also was a fervent Catholic in Hong Kong. It was altogether a toxic combination. The convent liberated me enough so that I knew quite early on that the roles of the dutiful daughter, the wise wife, the good mother were not scripted for me.

Once I remarked to my playmates that I would love to be enrolled in a boarding school. My main desire was to have other schoolmates to interact with. My subliminal desire was to be away from the stern disciplines of my mother. The mother of my playmates heard this conversation and reported it to my mother. The result was that I received a severe lecture accompanied by at least two days of silent anger — it was inconceivable that, being an only child, I could wish to live away from my parents. Did I not realize that my wish implied that I was not treated well at home? It was also considered an embarrassment as the wish was publicized to outsiders. My mother should have recognized the signs even then. When I was no older than ten, I was looking for a kind of freedom that she had never dreamt of or understood.

Thus, unlike other children, I loved school. And that I went to a convent school was the saving of me. My mother was strict, emotional, and humiliated me fairly regularly by slapping me or beating me (corporal punishment was not an unusual way to bring up children in her generation and before; and child abuse was not a concept then. Many children in Chinese culture, and no doubt in other cultures, were caned or slapped for disobedience and problematic behaviour, and the majority survived these parental treatments. I had witnessed young friends of mine accepting being belted by their parents and they seemed to be well adjusted adults. But I didn't like being punished, either psychologically or physically, and often had childish fantasies of revenge. I longed for the day when I could be independent). The nuns were detached, never laid a finger on me, and most important of all, allowed me free reign of my imagination and rewarded me for it.

Not all religious orders are alike. I recently read an essay by Brian Titley on the Sisters of Mercy and Sisters of Charity in Ireland who operated asylums for women of so-called dubious morals. Titley called these nuns "sadistic." Nor were these asylums medieval institutions dedicated to controlling women and their activities, because they were still operating in the 70s. But at the time when young Irish women were still incarcerated in asylums without due process, without recourse to legal rights, I was being educated by a very different set of nuns.

The Maryknoll Sisters began as an American mission to spread Catholicism in East Asia. Maryknoll Sisters School was established in Hong Kong when missionaries became persona non grata in communist China. Among some of the nuns who taught me, there were a few who felt great bitterness at the communist government because they were more or less kicked out of China. Interestingly, they were also the worst disciplinarians. Luckily, the nuns whom I had most contact with — those who taught literature, language, and Biblical exegesis — were imported from the States. They didn't undergo the physical hardship and humiliation their older colleagues might have — they were generally younger, more idealistic than religious, and liberal. If they weren't nuns, they would have been anti-Vietnam protesters on the streets.

Until the early 70s, the Maryknoll nuns wore the full black and white traditional habits with wimple, thus ironically mirroring the Islamic custom that dictates women not to show hair or bare limbs, a custom that the West now finds objectionable. They lived on the upper floor of the school, looked after by a few servants who were allowed entry to their domestic space. They were always clean and tidy, and it was a minor excitement for the students when the nun who taught Chemistry had to tie back her flowing habit in order to work with the Bunsen burner and other equipments. (With so much skin coverage, a glimpse of Sister J.M.'s bare wrist sent us into girlish giggles and this revelation was much discussed during recess.) Some nuns were ugly; some were beautiful, especially the one who taught us literature. She went by the name of a saint, but after Vatican II, she reverted back to her given name and turned out to be of American Irish background. She had rosy porcelain skin and short reddish hair. Tall and statuesque, she carried an air of authority effortlessly. Sister H. loved cinema and organized outings for the chosen few, who would accompany her to see matinees at the Lee Theatre, followed by tea afterwards.

My "best" friend, who turned out not to be such a best friend after graduation, was besotted with a nun who taught sciences and played the guitar. She — the nun — was striking in a Hilary Swank way: very chiselled and strong features, very piercing eyes, and was more masculine than feminine. The two of them were inseparable and there was the usual gossip (we were totally naïve), but I don't remember the term lesbianism was ever mentioned. I think during those months when the two of them were spending a lot of time together, I was used as a kind of chaperone or alibi, though I have no concrete memory of any particular instance.

After we left Maryknoll, both of us went to Canadian universities, although on the two different coasts of the country. We met up once but we were virtual strangers to each other. I never had the courage to ask my friend if she still kept in touch with her favourite nun.

So, my concepts of womanhood were formed by my mother and the nuns. From my mother, I was forced to believe that a woman must marry and have a family; the husband must be the provider; the provider must also take care of the in-laws and have their approval; the provider was expected to be Chinese. Sex was never discussed, although my grandmother did warn me against being touched by strange men (what about men who were not strangers?). Virginity was so important that every time I went out without my mother, I had to provide details of my outing — where I was, what I did, who was I with. Parents no doubt can still relate to this kind of panic; but I also believe that today's parents would try to find a way to balance the inquisitional instinct with respect for their teenager's rights. I suppose I was also angered by the assumption of wrongdoing these investigative sessions implied.

From the nuns, I learned that a woman could be empowered through education. That the education profession could be just as fulfilling and respectable as being a wife and a mother. That a woman could be fascinating even if she wore the same outfit every day. That a woman did not need to wear designer clothes and a Rolex watch in order to be respected in society. That a community of women within an institutional context could be a viable way of living. That one could appreciate literature even if one were Chinese. That there was an elegant way of living without resorting to the rat race outside of the convent. That sex could be discussed, and even written about (we read D.H. Lawrence's *Rainbow* with Sister H.!)

After spending years at Maryknoll, I chose to follow their way to empowerment instead of my mother's. It was not the nuns' intention to alienate their Chinese students from their families, and to my knowledge, none of my fellow students felt the way I did. But if one recalls the purpose of the missionary project in general, then Maryknoll has indeed managed to teach me to privilege the West over the East. To my parents' credit, they insisted that I continued studying Chinese History and Literature. Thus I am not totally alienated from my cultural roots. I only preferred the Western intellectual path because it promised me an adulthood of freedom.

Even then, I was never free of my mother, not even in university and after. The nuns were gone and I never had the opportunity to show them the fruits of their labour in my achievements. On the other hand, in my mother's eye, I had succeeded intellectually but failed in every way — not the wife of a wealthy Chinese, not the mother of a family, not the close and loving companion of her own mother. Though of late these maternal laments are muted, I cannot forget how my triumph is my mother's defeat.

In an illuminating discussion between a colleague and me, we agreed that I am writing about my mother both as an academic and a daughter. I have never known my mother as a friend, although I can intellectually understand her as a woman. In contrast, she has never treated me as a grown woman. The question is, can we possibly write outside of a fixed relational experience? Another question is that of betrayal. In his article for *The Guardian*, "When art imitates life," Sarfraz Manzoor suggests that "for those who choose to write about their loved ones, a sliver of generosity might [...] be welcome" (February 17, 2007). I have thought much about how to represent my mother without betrayal. In Chinese culture, one does not wash family dirty linens in public. The culture is one of constraint and reserve. Furthermore, in Chinese culture, one does not criticize one's parents. My solution, successful or not, is to position myself as an outsider looking at a relationship between a mother and a daughter, using my memories as tools for analysis. I also put my mother within a cultural context — her actions were acculturated and she was not an exception in whatever she did and did not do. Obviously actions led to consequences, and these consequences could not be ignored. That applies to any parent-child relationship.

This chapter does not exhaust my analysis of the mother-daughter relationship I am involved in, but more personal anecdotes, more complex evaluations of how the relationship has evolved or not developed, more theorizing on how cultural environments have affected a relationship that is conventionally believed to be fundamental and unassailable — these must wait for another book.

Deaths in the Family

Family obligations were part of the Chinese culture that I consistently fought against. Since one couldn't argue against values accepted by over a billion people for thousands of years, I tend to take the cowardly but expedient way out. For instance, I would arrange to attend a conference somewhere else when some member of the family got married. I would leave the city rather than be involved with birthdays, weddings, funerals, or visiting relatives. Unlike my mother, who truly believes that blood is thicker than water and no strangers can ever play a more important role in one's life than one's relatives, I find my extended families, maternal and paternal, complete strangers with whom I cannot hold a prolonged and meaningful conversation. My knowledge of my relationship to them — Chinese culture has very elaborate ways of tabulating familial relationships, and there are specific terms for someone who is the second son of the second son of one's paternal grandfather — is always vague.

The last time I saw all my relatives — my father's many cousins and their many wives and children (some men with more than one wife); all my mother's siblings — would be during my father's funeral. I was sixteen. The Chinese tradition cares more about the dead than the living. Everyone was consumed by the arrangements of the funeral, which consisted both of the Chinese rituals and the Catholic ones. No one asked me how I felt, the psychological effect on a teenager whose father died a long and lingering death. The truth was, I felt rotten not just because my father died, but that the whole situation was, to a Westernized me, deeply disturbing without the benefit of catharsis.

First of all, my mother was hysterical about 95 percent of the time during the three-day vigil we had to keep in a Chinese funeral home. To me, she was a public spectacle in her endless tears and loud mourning.

(She believed that the more visible the mourning, the more authentic the emotions.) I have to concur with Elizabeth II (in the film *The Queen*) in her attitude that we do not grieve in public, that mourning should be a private matter and one should present to the world a silent dignity. Unfortunately, in Chinese culture, grief is public. Hence the tortuous vigil, the awful mourning gowns we had to wear — they were hooded sacks that made me look like a KKK member, the stream of relatives and friends we had to greet and whom I had never met, the hearse that rolled in first gear through the street to the cemetery (did we really walk from the funeral home in North Point to the Catholic cemetery in Happy Valley?), the mass held in the cemetery chapel, and, at last, the graveside ritual. It was August; the day was searing hot; the chapel was tiny and we packed it completely. It was a wonder that no one fainted from the smothering heat. I was directed by someone to throw the first fistful of soil onto the coffin while my mother was attempting to throw herself into the grave. Then as I tried to brush my muddy hands, someone else stopped me and said that was not done. So I stood around glumly and sullenly, watching various relatives restraining my mother, who was wailing as loudly as possible, and surreptitiously wiped my hands on the KKK gown.

One would have thought that this should provide closure to the death of an ordinary family man. But my mother prolonged the lamenting to extraordinary length, in accordance to Chinese tradition. We had to wear black and white for three or six months; then we could only wear sombre colours, such as browns and navy. We visited the grave almost daily. I suppose my mother was inconsolable. And I didn't have the tenderness in me to console her, since all I could think of was how we had to depend on each other now, with no intermediary, with no third person to diffuse any situation. Worse, she would have no one else to lavish her attention on. My father's death became the beginning of a long prison sentence for me.

During the serious mourning period — six months, I think — I wasn't allowed to go out with friends, to go to movies, and whenever anyone mentioned my father, my mother would break down, in the privacy of our home or in public. She was going through a period of self-flagellation, which added to her intense misery. She reviewed the days and nights before my father's death (which involved months), and blamed herself for every harsh word she had said to him, every "no" she had uttered to his wishes (not always very reasonable ones); every argument she had incited. She remembered aloud all the good things about my father — his generosity, his gentleness, his good taste, his affection for his family. In my cynical way, though I was only a teenager, I thought the energy would have been much better spent treating him with love and patience when he was alive.

From this experience I evolved for myself the motto in life: take responsibility for my actions and no regrets.

My second intimate experience with death occurred when my grandmother died in Vancouver. All her living children and many of her grandchildren showed up, except for her second son. I missed the mass (and I cannot remember what excuse I made) but showed up for the burial. We all wore the traditional black cotton mourning gowns that an aunt brought from Hong Kong. At the graveside, after the coffin was lowered and before the bulldozer started shovelling the soil into the grave, my mother told everyone to kneel down. It was a testament to the filial obedience in Chinese culture that no one even thought of disagreeing with her. I had an absurd image of the scene: in a windy patch of ground in a huge cemetery in Vancouver, about fifteen Chinese, all dressed in black hooded gowns, knelt before a dirty yellow earth-moving machine and bowed their heads as the machine went about its business. I don't know what my other relatives thought of the scene. On cue it started to rain.

(A more recent example of how the rituals of death are more important than the living person was demonstrated again when my mother's favourite sister died in Hong Kong. My mother wanted me to make sure that my cousin in Hong Kong would buy wreaths for us. I was more concerned about the emotional and mental state of my cousin, who would be dealing with the funeral and other arrangements on her own, without the support of any of her relatives, who are scattered outside of Hong Kong. If I had wanted to cause more grief for my mother, I should have asked her why our wreaths were more important than the well-being of my cousin.)

Cemeteries

I am looking at a map of Hong Kong Island. It always comes as a surprise to find great swathes of land that are marked as green space: Braemar Hill, Jardine's Lookout, the Peak, Pok Fu Lam Shan. And in the area between Central and North Point, the relentlessly urban streets are interspersed with green patches: Victoria Park, the hill surrounding the Hong Kong Stadium, Happy Valley racecourse, and walking up the slope of Stubbs Road, a visitor can find herself in spaces that resemble English country lanes, except for the highrises that loom and dwarf the arbutus trees that are picturesquely unkempt on the hillsides. These neighbourhoods that are built on the hill, with street names such as Magazine Gap Road, Kennedy Road, Bowen Road, were formerly the preserves of the colonialists. Somerset Maugham characters would live around these winding roads, coddled by their amahs and chauffeurs and cooks. Now, wealthy Chinese park their Mercedes and Rolls Royce in the front courts, while their maids from the Philippines or Indonesia take the children to nearby playgrounds in the afternoon.

Would I have such an affinity for different built environments if I hadn't grown up in the very diverse neighbourhood of Causeway Bay? I virtually grew up with Victoria Park as my playground. For six days a week, the bus took me pass the Caroline Hill area where the soccer stadium was, along the Wong Nai Chung Road that embraced the racecourse, up the slope of Blue Pool Road, lined by two-storey single family houses with Art Deco architectural motifs, and deposited me on Holly Road, from where I walked to Maryknoll Sisters School. Like the mansions in Mid-Levels, the school was built on land that was formerly part of the rocky hillside that made up Hong Kong. By virtue of the economics of the real estate of that whole area, there were no poor people near the school until one moved eastward towards Tai Hang and the illegal shacks that were the flip side of the posh addresses in Happy Valley. I might have developed a different sense of spatial aesthetics if my parents had lived in the more congested Shau Kei Wan, essentially a fishing village built into densely populated tenements, or the less salubrious Sai Ying Pun, formerly an area of godowns and warehouses and factories of pungent preserved fish, equally pungent pickled vegetables, and so on.

As it were, I learned to love green spaces, houses with interesting architectural details, historical buildings, tree-lined streets, not because I understood urban design at that time in my life, but because they were markers of the better social classes — bankers, professionals, and most of all, non-Chinese. Growing up, I knew little of the workers who made their living through home factories, fishing, hard labours, except when my mother took me to our family tailor. He lived in Shau Kei Wan and a visit to him entailed a long tram ride, then a walk through dirt lanes into what must have been some village that was on the verge of being urbanized. Our tailor rented the upper floor of some Dickensian shack. The ground floor sold preserved eggs, black bean paste, and other grocery items necessary to a Chinese kitchen. To reach our tailor, we had to climb a propped up ladder; then we emerged into the second floor of the shack. My mother started using this particular tailor during World War II and had stayed loyal to him, though he was really not fashionable anymore. He made Western suits (a kind of dowdy jacket and skirt ensemble) for mother and me, though not for my father, who had his own tailor. For the traditional cheongsam, my mother went to a different tailor; this man had escaped Shanghai either during the war, or after the Communist Party took over China. These visits were an adventure to me, but it also introduced me to the idea that I lived in a pretty nice neighbourhood. And that that difference must be because we belonged to a better social class.

I knew about the cemeteries of course, even before my father was buried there, since anyone on a tram that travelled westward on Wong Nai Chung Road would see, if she sat on the upper level, the exotic entrance to the Parsee cemetery, then the dour Protestant or colonial cemetery, then the more flamboyant Catholic cemetery, and finally, the mysterious Muslim cemetery that looked like an abandoned garden. A guidebook to Hong Kong would never tell you that the cemeteries in Happy Valley are lovely spots to spend an afternoon in on hot summer days.

As mentioned, my father was buried in the Catholic cemetery. When he died, we managed to buy a plot that was not too far up the hill. One entered the central lane and turned right at the chapel, then up a flight of steps and there would be my father's grave. The gravestone is pink marble, with gold-filled lettering written by an expert calligrapher. No English. Behind the grave is a frangipani tree. In season, the tree sheds the most fragrant yellow blossoms. While we were still living in Hong Kong, my mother and I would gather these creamy yellow flowers and leave them in a container on the grave. We took the leftover blooms home. Though the frangipani tree provided little shade, there were other trees in the cemetery, such as banyan. Except for festive days there was little traffic in the cemetery. It was a pocket of silent calm. Richard and I used to walk around looking at gravestones as if we were window-shopping. When tired of commenting on the designs of gravestones or names of the deceased, we would sit down under a tree and chat about culture or poetry in its shade. Maybe it was these conversations that provided the lingering romantic image I have of cemeteries in general.

Who can forget the wonderful last cemetery scene in *The Third Man*, as a heartbroken and beautiful Alida Valli, in a belted trench coat and fedora, hands in pockets, walks by a waiting and contrite Joseph Cotton, after Orson Welles's Harry Lime is buried in Vienna? I like visiting cemeteries when I travel. The most enchanting and intimate one is in Reykjavik, right in the city centre, flowing with flowering trees and ornamented by iron fences around some graves of important citizens. Sometimes cemeteries are political statements for obvious reasons. In Berlin, architect Peter Eisenman designed a Jewish monument that resembles a cemetery near the German parliament, the Reichstag. On a hot sunny day, to walk around the shadeless place is torture, as is no doubt the intention of the architect. (In the summer of 2006, I was crossing the road in Potsdamer Platz when an elderly Jewish woman asked me for directions to the Eisenman monument. I was so surprised that someone would ask me directions in German in Berlin that I gave her inaccurate information and worried afterwards if she managed to find the place in the insufferable heat.)

In another area in Berlin, on Grosse Hamburger Strasse, is the group of statues that commemorate the oldest Jewish cemetery of the city, established in 1672. It was destroyed during World War II, and the area, apart from the park, is walled in. The guidebook informs me that behind the wall could be found the tombstone of Moses Mendelssohn. When I walked up to the guards, who looked like Mossad agents in their khaki mufti and aviator sunglasses, to ask for admission, I was told flatly that the public was not allowed in. Later, I found that a school for Jewish children is attached to the former cemetery.

In 2005, my mother and I made our way, under a merciless sun, to my father's grave. We paid one of the enterprising people who sold pails of water to grave visitors for some water for the flowers. We were soaking and I was hyperventilating, from the stress of visiting the cemetery with my mother and from the weather. She talked to the marble headstone as if my father were somehow plugged in, while I shuffled on the side, after bowing three times to my father's smiling picture as etiquette required. I tried to remember those days when she forced me to visit the grave, treating each neglected afternoon as a major transgression. Then when I started meeting Richard at the cemetery, I could openly tell her where I was and felt avenged that she was pleased, but for the wrong reason. Some of that sullen teenager was in me still that afternoon, although more than three decades have passed. I could not remember any details of my secret afternoons with Richard. But it couldn't have been so hot in the 70s, could it? As we left the cemetery, I flagged down a taxi, ignoring my mother's remonstrance, and was vastly relieved as I felt the air-conditioning in the car drying out my sweating skin. No apotheosis; just discomfort.

Football (soccer) and Other Obsessions

I watched all television shows in English. That way, I managed to learn to understand English very well for someone with my kind of background. Rawhide, Bonanza, all the BBC shows, even golfing tournaments and wrestling. But I didn't learn to love football (soccer) through television.

My earliest memory of a football match was when I was three or four. My father took me to games regularly. His seat was at the very top of the old stadium. To avoid my being crushed by the fans when we lined up to get in, my father put me on his shoulders. We watched the local teams, and we listened to big matches, such as the World Cup, on the radio. Though we had a television in the 60s, I don't remember match broadcasts on the English-language channel.

Another reason I developed an affection for football was the location of the stadium. Caroline Hill Road was the midpoint between Maryknoll (school) and Bayview Mansion (home). To go home from school, I took the Happy Valley bus. In my last years at Maryknoll, some of us would get off at the bottom of the hill where Maryknoll was and walked along the east arm of Wong Nai Chung Road that more or less wraps around the Happy Valley track for horse racing. Then we turned up Broadlink Road, passed St. Margaret's Church (my mother's local parish), and walked to the intersection of Caroline Hill Road and Hoi Ping Road. This is an area where expatriates also frequented, mainly because of its proximity to the hillside neighbourhoods of Happy Valley. The shops around here in the 60s catered to a more Westernized clientele: coffee shops, record stores, shops where one could buy Wrangler and Levi jeans, etc. As already mentioned, Sister H. used to take a few of the "girls" to see films at the Lee Garden Theatre (gone), followed by tea somewhere on Hysan Avenue. There were posh apartments around this area, with doormen in uniforms.

I have since been to the new stadium, once to watch Michael Chang play tennis and most recently, to watch Hong Kong play Manchester United. It was a hot August day, with afternoon temperature hovering around 33 degrees Celsius. I bought a mid-ranged ticket and was seated between Chinese men who were wearing only shorts and sweating profusely. The match was deeply uninteresting in that the Hong Kong team featured no international stars the way Man United could. But the Chinese put up a good fight and the score was 0 – 0 after the first half. I walked around during the break and noticed that the fans were all Chinese, with the majority men. After Man United scored in the second half and the outcome was never in doubt, I left early to beat the exiting crowd. In order to get a taxi, I had to walk all the way to Hoi Ping Road. It was suffocatingly hot and I was desperate to get back to my air-conditioned hotel room. So desperate that I elbowed a man who towered over me and was in the process of opening the back door of a taxi out of the way. The taxi driver was not only amused by my aggressiveness, but also by my knowledge of football. We discussed the game all the way to the hotel, and I told him about my years of following the sport when I was living in Hong Kong.

In the 60s, the players would have finished practice around mid-afternoon. They could be spotted walking back from the stadium to their hotel apartment around the Lee Garden area. Like teenage fans from the world over, we followed our favourite players; but we were too timid to ask for an autograph. The players were probably quite aware of the gaggle of giggling teenage girls in school uniform "stalking" them. Rangers were my favourite Hong Kong team because they imported players from Britain. Of course now I know that these players were the ones who couldn't make the Barclay Premiership or even the first or second league, as they are called now. Or they were near the end of their careers and were sold to play in outposts like Hong Kong. But in the 60s and I in my teens, these foreigners were exotic to me — they had long flowing hair; they were taller and stronger than the Chinese footballers; and their teams often won. For me, then, a winning record was more important than national loyalty.

(I announced this unpatriotic attitude in a very public way. In the 70s a Chinese from Taiwan was a top athlete and competed well internationally. Then she married her coach, who was an American. Or at least, he was a Westerner. Chinese media condemned this marriage, somehow seeing it as her betrayal of her national and racial identity. I wrote to one of the Hong Kong newspapers and defended her, claiming that she had the right to marry whomever she wanted. My letter was published, followed by the editor's response. I should have kept the newspaper — my first publication — because my letter showed how "Westernized" I already was at eighteen or nineteen.)

Football, therefore, means many things to me. Most obviously, it is an enjoyable spectator sport. Because I was introduced to it at an early age, it never occurred to me that being a football fan wasn't a particularly feminine activity. Watching football was also linked to some of my fondest memories — time spent with my father but not with my mother; time spent after school but before going home. When my father was seriously ill, we had little to talk about except football. We followed the 1966 World Cup together; we both willed England to win the tournament. With what little energy and enthusiasm left in him, my father cheered every goal scored and lamented every missed volley. Football belonged to the masculine domain that I preferred to that of housework and kitchen chores.

Another reason for my football fandom only becomes clear to me once I have started to study constructions of gender and ethnic stereotypes. Footballers come in all shapes and sizes, which make them more interesting as athletes than, for example, a tour bicyclist, whose torso must carry as little fat as possible but has to have massive thighs to generate lower body strength. Because of the global nature of football, one can study national stereotypes and media representations with accessible samples, given that one can find East Asian, African, South American, and all European ethnicities in European football leagues. The footballers I admired as a teenager also represented a tabooed masculinity — they were Westerners; they were intriguing and exotic; they were dangerous. We were brought up with the usual warning against Western men, who were sexually rapacious and immoral. (I wonder if that was the reason Maryknoll never hired Western male teachers, though we were taught by two Chinese men?)

Now Chinese men could be perceived as potent and powerful and even as sex symbols internationally. Look at Tony Leung and Andy Lau, introduced to Western audiences through *Infernal Affairs*; or Chow Yun-fat in Ang Lee's *Crouching Tiger, Hidden Dragon*. Or the many Jet Li Hollywood vehicles. But when I was growing up, the sex symbols were predominantly Western — Steven McQueen, Paul Newman, and so on. I could not remember any Chinese film stars who had the same media attention outside of East Asia. (However, I should mention that in a rather schizophrenic way, my parents only liked Western films and I was brought up on *Cleopatra* and *El Cid*, as well as the James Bond franchise.

With this constant diet of Western men being held up as the standard of masculinity, no wonder I admired footballers and not ping pong players.)

One of my other obsessions was film and television. As mentioned already, I watched all British and American television programmes available. I thought the motorcycle diaries of *Then Came Bronson* very romantic — a man who could have an adventure in American heartland weekly in different cities; I envied the lives of families in *Father Knows Best* or *Peyton Place* — roomy houses to live in, white picket fences protecting a flowering garden. I especially loved the wide streets with NO people and NO trash. (Forty years later I am living the lifestyle that I admired so much in Hong Kong — though it was not by any conscious effort.) I stayed up late and watched episodes based on Somerset Maugham's Southeast Asian short stories. My knowledge of English was not sophisticated enough to understand the drama between these British colonialists and their failed lives in Singapore or Melaka, but I understood enough to find the fraught relationships between people — ponderously psychoanalysed and then dramatized — highly entertaining. More than anything, these characters' suffering (for they are usually unhappy beings forced by circumstances to live in exile from the "empire") made me feel better and lifted me out of my own unhappiness.

Maids in Hong Kong

One of my mother's two sisters died recently. I saw her last during a summer research visit. At that time, she was in a wheelchair and was tended to by a maid from some Indonesian village, who had a young son back home. And possibly an unemployed husband. The rest of my family was not particularly interested in her life and history, unlike me, who saw her as another sign of Hong Kong economically colonizing poorer Asian countries. A sign that I noticed even in the 50s.

We were not wealthy by any means, and since my mother never ceased to reiterate how hard it was to make money and how essential it was to keep it, I grew up with an inferiority complex regarding wealthy people and a superiority complex regarding those who belonged to social classes considered lower than ours. Add to my mother's dire warning of imminent poverty the nostalgic account of the landowning family my father belonged to and his pedigree, it got a bit confusing for a child. To what class did my family belong? We seemed to have wealthy friends. Whenever we visited them, I was embarrassed because we came by taxi (or even by bus!) instead of our own car. And I always felt that their servants were patronizing us because we were so obviously poorer than their employers. (An enduring memory — a woman friend of my mother's lived in a multi-room single-family house with maids and gardener. She drove a Jaguar E-type while her husband had a chauffeur for his own posh car. This "auntie" wore a coat of leopard skin in winter, stiletto heels, and when we were to go out together, my mother and I would sit around in her huge bedroom and watch her choose her outfit from one of the many built-in wardrobes that lined the room. From time to time, depending on her whims, she would give me jewellery as presents. I still wear a string of pearls that I got as a teenager after my father died. I always presumed that, being cynical at a young age, we went out with her because she always paid the bills.)

The only time when we could afford a servant was when we were living on Electricity Road. I can't remember how my parents treated her. My father was probably indifferent. In his own way he was socially arrogant. My mother would have been exacting. I showed very little respect. Though I was only three or four, I instinctively knew that this woman wasn't part of the family. She didn't eat with us. She lived in the back of the apartment in some makeshift cubby-hole. She had to take orders from my mother. We never had a conversation with her. I knew nothing about her personal life. I don't even remember her name now. It always puzzles me when colonialists write warmly of their native servants, because the reality of the master-servant relationship would have precluded intimate knowledge and genuine communication. And why would a servant, especially one of a non-Western race, feel unreserved loyalty towards an employer who represented the prejudice of a society that ranked money and skin colour as signs of superiority?

My next experience of maids was when we had the partial service of the maids of our landlord's family. The older one was an absolute dragon — she was snobbish; she was a terrible gossip; and she was fearless. My most vivid memory of her was when she killed a mouse with a chopstick. She had the responsibility of looking after the four children of our landlord and his wife; the more menial tasks of cleaning and shopping were undertaken by a recent refugee from mainland communist China. The young woman, more a teenager, was good-natured but untutored in the ways of the big city. The children, including me, often made fun of her mercilessly. Sometimes we allowed her to play with us; but we never forgot that, though she should be at school like us, she was only a servant. There was no social awareness regarding the rights and wrongs of hiring someone at a very low wage to do one's dirty chores, especially when that person had no recourse to personal betterment. When this young woman got pregnant, she was immediately fired. There was no compassion; no talk of helping her; no references to any social network that could help her. And I didn't give her another thought after she was gone.

After I met my aunt's Indonesian maid, I asked my mother for details of her employment. How much was she paid? Where did she come from? Where did she sleep in my aunt's very small apartment? She was paid the standard rate. She worked six days a week, and since she stayed in a bunk bed in my aunt's apartment, she practically worked twenty-four hours a day. She came from a poor village and she was the only wage earner in the family. I hated the dinner at which we all pretended that she was one of the family while she had to pay attention to my aunt's needs — I couldn't stand the artificial relationship between the rest of my family and this woman. I don't think my family could have acted differently. There is no social script that allows for dialogue between those who could afford a servant and those who have no other choices but be a servant. I told myself that, at least, my aunt needed one because she was in a wheelchair, not because she thought she was too good to wash her own dishes and do her own laundry.

On my aunt's maid's day off, she joined the tens of thousands of other maids in Hong Kong, mainly from the Philippines, Malaysia, and Indonesia, who took over several main thoroughfares in the central district. These underpaid and exploited women would put down blankets on kerbsides and crossroads, and groups would form. They chatted and exchanged news. They cut hair and wrote letters home. They ate home-cooked meals. They performed on makeshift stages their native songs. When I was there in 2005, I discovered that even bus routes changed on Sunday so that these women could have their own day's outing till ten at night on these streets without motor traffic. The Hong Kong people seemed not to find this phenomenon unusual. Sociologists have published essays about it. I walked amongst them when I had to cross the harbour via the Star Ferry, or when I went to the IFC Towers to shop and to use the internet cafe. The maids never staged their social outings inside malls. Thus, class and class differences were clearly represented — inside the mall, the Hong Kong Chinese shopped at Bulgari jewellery, Lanvin couture; outside, on Chater Road, on Queen's Road Central, in front of the Mandarin Hotel, in front of the Landmark, where Christian Dior had a Hong Kong branch, women from poor Southeast Asian countries sat and performed daily practices that they normally would at home, on the one day when they didn't have to come at the beck and call of their Chinese employers.

A colleague from Hong Kong University told me that she hired two sisters who were illegal migrants (I can't remember from where) to clean her apartment and do her laundry once a week. She said she didn't really need any one to do the housework. Her apartment was less than 500 square feet. But it was a way to let these women have some money. She always made sure that she was out of the apartment when the women were around. Her Western and liberal social conscience made her feel uncomfortable to witness someone ironing her Marks and Spencer knickers and dusting her books.

Expats I Knew

Actually, I only knew one expat "well," given the cultural and racial narrowness of my world.

His name was Richard, just like the Joni Mitchell song.

I met him at a poetry recording at the Hong Kong branch of BBC.

I entered several poems and two were chosen, though I wasn't the winner. Then I was asked to come to the studio to read my own poems and was given a little cheque. My first pay cheque and I was seventeen.

There was a group of us, all aspiring or pretentious poets. Some were Chinese and some were expatriates.

We were listening to one particular Chinese contestant reading hers and Richard whispered to me, "Very Eliot." He must have introduced himself to me and sat next to me outside the recording room.

I didn't know who Eliot was, not even George Eliot, never mind T.S. (Obviously Maryknoll's literature curriculum was not perfect!)

I developed a crush on him instantly.

Later, he told me that he got a degree from King's College, Cambridge. (Of the dreaming spires! I learned that from a crossword puzzle in *Times Literary Supplement* while reading in the British Council Reading Room.)

He was in Hong Kong as an expat teacher and was living at Caritas, a dormitory run by the religious group. The building on Caine Road was still there in 2005. It didn't look at all glamorous, not the way it was in my memory.

It couldn't have been Richard as a person that was the attraction, in that my family situation was such that I couldn't possibly believe that we could develop a relationship with each other.

But he represented literature, British culture and tradition, ideas, a world outside of Hong Kong. A world that I read about.

Richard took me out but he didn't make much money and we spent many meetings sitting at a rooftop café by the harbour, nursing a glass of tepid tonic water. The ice melted in the scorching sun and the glass was as wet outside as inside.

But he was impressed with my general and literary knowledge, because his students were so inferior in their English and their reading background, he told me.

He probably saw me as a bright student that he wished he could have in his class. I met him in my last year at Maryknoll. We saw each other for another summer.

My last anarchic act at Maryknoll was to introduce Richard to my favourite nuns at the convent. I must have given them some story about him — some visiting scholar from Cambridge researching educational system in Hong Kong?

My fellow Maryknollers were agog.

They thought Richard was going to get a tour of the nuns' quarters, an area no one, except the servants, was allowed.

We had long conversations about poetry, about existentialism, about art.

I was introduced to Ingmar Bergman and saw *Shame* with Richard.

Nothing else happened, in that we didn't sleep together — there was no place for us to engage in any real intimacy.

I took him home once and my mother went berserk. After he left, I spent days explaining myself. There were tears. There were temperamental flare-ups. There were vulgar accusations from her and contemptuous retorts from me.

Richard must have traumatized my mother so much that she never approved of a single non-Chinese man I introduced to her in Canada. I stopped doing that several years ago and my private life remained private even to my mother. Especially my mother.

In a way, then, my first attempt to "date" a non-Chinese and to normalize it with my family also traumatized me — the first lesson should have alerted me, and probably did, that nothing concerning interracial relationships in my life would be easy.

The last summer I saw Richard, he was engaged to a Texan woman. She was tall, like him, and had long blond hair.

Life was supremely unfair in my mind in those days. I was short and had badly cut black hair. I was short-sighted and plump.

If I wore the jeans that Richard's fiancée wore, I would have to cut off half of the length.

The only "gift" I had was keen observation.

I also had a good memory.

But Richard chose one of his kind — a white woman who drawled.

As a parting gift, Richard gave me an Oxford dictionary.

That was the way I attracted him — as a student more than a potential lover. Well, lover seems an overly romantic term.

I still can't see what he saw in me — one of many Hong Kong Chinese adolescent girls who developed a crush on some expat because he was exotic. Which was what I was and what he was.

Richard introduced me to a world that was closed to me, in spite of the prestige of being a Maryknoller. I had no non-Chinese friends. I never went to any Westernized places such as the Godown (a club and restaurant) or the Foreign Correspondence Club, both places I have since visited as a visiting scholar from Canada. The irony!

Richard naturally knew the expats network and he took me to clubs where everyone smoked and gossiped about friends in an accent that I only ever heard on the BBC or in films. He called one woman a bitch and a snob because she was going on about some social function in London that she should have attended. Then he told me his sister was a deb the coming season. I didn't understand at all what he was saying. Or for that matter, any of the conversations going on around me. I smiled insipidly and pretended. Most of these occasions were quite boring because I was excluded from any conversations and no one bothered to explain things to me.

(I have since read Le Carré's *The Honourable Schoolboy* and can attest to the authentic tone and inanity of the British expats as portrayed in the novel.)

I didn't smoke or drink either. But I persisted in going to these social evenings because it was so different from having dinner with my relatives in some Chinese restaurant, where everyone ate heartily and steadily but no one stopped, leaned back in some upholstered armchair, with a gin and tonic in one hand and a cigarette in the other, discoursing on the latest Ingmar Bergman film or the latest Iris Murdoch novel. Or flirted.

Even the lighting in these places was different. These clubs and bars Richard introduced me to were lit in some mysterious amber twilight, where people looked relaxed and thoughtful. An illusion, of course. But in Chinese places, the fluorescent lights were full on, everyone's wrinkles and worries were evident. Every morsel of food stuck between teeth. Every spot of tea on the tablecloth.

I chose the amber twilight. But I also knew that I was an outsider, even though I understood and spoke enough English to get by.

In retrospect, I must have struck the servers of these expats places as a very inexperienced hooker, with my inexpertly applied lipstick and micro-mini. I learned, through following Richard around his expats circle, that a Chinese woman must maintain a tremendous amount of dignity and elegance when she is socializing with Western men. This poise would offset the inequality between racialized gender stereotypes — what I call the Susie Wong syndrome.

But I knew nothing of this at the age of seventeen.

In 2005 I went to Hong Kong to attend an international conference at the University of Hong Kong. I was a tenured associate professor, several social steps above the innocent and gauche teenager in the 70s. But I still packed a carefully planned wardrobe; I spent a ridiculous amount of money to get my hair coloured and cut; I maintained a friendly but aloof attitude during the conference. As if anyone would care.

But I did.

(I also sometimes pretended that I only spoke English, a very childish gesture. It backfired the day when I went to a hairstylist on D'Aguilar Street. I started by playing the role of a tourist. The exchanges were all in English. Unfortunately, the very pleasant young men who ran the place spoke really poor English, which begged the question: why did they start a business in an expat area? While I tried to give precise instructions in simple English, the stylist obviously didn't really understand me. The outcome wasn't disastrous; but it wasn't what I wanted. I could have reverted to Cantonese at some point in the two-hour session, but that would have offended the stylist and made myself look ridiculous.)

I cared so much about whether I was treated with respect in Hong Kong that I went to the Mandarin Oriental quite a bit for lunch and drinks during my stay.

I frequented a chain bookstore that stocked books in English and bought many.

I shopped at Lane Crawford, a posh department store.

I walked around the Mid-Levels neighbourhood every day.

I took taxis.

In other words, for the duration of my stay over the summer, I lived like an expat would have when I was on the fringe of his world. In 2005, I socialized with colleagues from the Hong Kong University, an occurrence that I would not have believed if someone had told me about it in the 70s.

My very British colleagues — HKU still seemed very British — were genial and, from what I could gather through conversations, apolitical.

But they have every reason not to want to get involved in the politics of Hong Kong and China.

Their pay is higher than university professors in North America.

They get living allowances. They get a bonus at the end of an academic year. A bonus!

They — many — have servants.

I was invited for lunch at the faculty club, on the top floor of a tower on campus that overlooked the harbour and Kowloon. The servers were Chinese. The professors were mainly non-Chinese. (Maybe the Chinese faculty members ate somewhere else.)

I reminded myself that I was an accredited member of this rarefied society; that, though I didn't have a membership, I was part of the culture and not some hanger-on.

It seems that decades ago, I chose my battle. I could have followed the path of total non-contact with Westerners, as all my Chinese friends and relatives followed. (A cousin recently married a non-Chinese Canadian. The family didn't protest but the father remained indifferent to his white son-in-law.) If one had to do business with a Westerner, then it was a different matter. But friendship beyond the socializing rituals of lunch and dinner was difficult; intimate relationships were impossible. I decided that I would keep my personal life a closed door to my Chinese side.

Let's follow another script.

Instead of succumbing to my mother's interdiction, I insisted on dating Richard. I would have to invite him to family dinners, with myself more or less the only interpreter. He would always have to eat Chinese food, since my family would not deign to cater to a foreigner. We would watch Chinese programmes on television if the family stayed home. Friends of my mother would exchange asides and glances, and my mother would feel deeply ashamed that her daughter was going out with a gweilo (a ghost-man), and one who wasn't even an executive at the Hong Kong and Shanghai Bank or some equally prestigious institution. There would be no attempt on the Chinese side to learn more about Richard. He would be barely tolerated. Every time after he left the scene, there would be lectures and harangues from my mother, and gentle admonition from relatives. And tears followed by threats. Furthermore, Richard would be bankrupted by the many bills he would have to pay to show that he was financially capable — gifts for me and my relatives, dinners out, cinemas, weekend trips to Macau or Repulse Bay for the day and so on.

That couldn't be the fate of all interracial relationships; but it would be the common one. I know people who managed to have a Western partner or husband. But these women had either a Westernized familial background already, or their partners were wealthy enough to override the racial stigma. Even in 2005, one didn't see many interracial couples on Hong Kong streets except in expat enclaves, such as the bar-lined Lan Kwai Fong neighbourhood. And when I encountered a big, hulking Westerner with a petite East Asian, or Southeast Asian woman, I still wondered about the nature of the relationship (the Susie Wong syndrome!). Just as my mother had taught me decades ago.

Book Places

The expat community might have been able to exclude me from any meaningful interaction with Westerners; but my mind was fully engaged with Western literature through voracious reading, while I took advantage of the few lending libraries open to Chinese and non-Chinese alike.

Dorothy L. Sayers

My love for literature was developed locationally. By that I mean that various writers or literary movements are inextricably linked, in my mind, to place. Take my passion for the detective mystery.

On a hot summer day in the early 70s, probably the last year at Maryknoll Sisters School, I read an advertisement in the *Hong Kong Standard* that so-and-so was selling off books at his apartment. The address was a side street off Kennedy Road. (I think I walked down that street when I was staying at the Mid-Levels YWCA in the summer of 2005.) It was a typically expatriate neighbourhood (still is) — the flats were usually rented out to Europeans or North Americans working downtown, or teaching in one of the numerous private schools (the equivalent of the British public school) located in mid-level Hong Kong: St. Stephen's, St. Joseph's, Sacred Heart, and of course, Hong Kong University on Pokfulam Road. I was seventeen, but felt no qualms going to some stranger's apartment to look at the books that were for sale. I think the book owner was leaving Hong Kong.

It must have been over 30 degrees Celsius, a typical bright July day (it might have been August). I dressed up to look like a person who was a serious reader — a cotton top, a straight skirt that almost reached the knees, and flats. I took two buses to get to this address. I had to walk down a steep hill, then up three floors to get to the books for sale. A good-looking South Asian man in his twenties was the seller. He smiled and then showed me a table covered with books and some boxes on the floor, and apologized that the selections had been picked over a bit. Then he politely stood by the window of the living room and pretended to be preoccupied with the view. At least, I don't remember his hovering around while I went slowly through the books laid out, ready to ensnare me and to enslave me for the rest of my reading life. (If this were an Eric Rohmer film, I would have been a gorgeous Parisian and the young man would have fallen madly in love with me. Alas, real life was not like that.)

I might have read a Christie mystery before that day, otherwise I wouldn't have picked out several Dorothy L. Sayers titles: *Clouds of Witnesses, Murder Must Advertise, The Unpleasantness of the Bellona Club*. I still have these copies, published in the 50s. They travelled with me from Hong Kong to Vancouver, from Vancouver to Edmonton, from Edmonton to Lethbridge, and no doubt eventually, from Lethbridge to Vancouver again. Sayers was the only author I bought. The quiet and polite young man smiled when I showed him my selection. "Ah, you are a Sayers fan, I see," he remarked in a posh British accent. (Somehow, I kept thinking that he looked like a young Pico Iyer.) The few books cost me no more than HK$20, but they came out of my spending money, of which I didn't have much. Yet, for over thirty years, I have unparalleled pleasure reading detective fiction, from the Conan Doyle classics to the latest from the Nordic countries. Maybe it was Sayers, or my British education, I only read either British or European mysteries, but very, very seldom American, and rarely, Canadian. (This reading practice also produces a reservoir of outmoded idioms that I use to amuse my friends: "I lost my rag" or "three sheets to the wind").

But more than any explanation, plausible or implausible, it was the romance of Sayers's world — not just the romance between the characters — but the world of wealth tempered by a fierce intelligence, and the writer's scrupulous desire to create a modern man, and later, a modern woman, in an essentially chauvinistic and patriarchal genre — that captivated me. And the white-clad, posh-accented, well located previous owner of these Sayers book seemed to affirm this world that filled my youthful fantasy world. It wasn't the individual per se, but his apartment, his books, his address, his obvious British background — I aspired to that world, living in teeming Causeway Bay, hardly ever had the chance to speak to an English person outside of school, dreaming of a life similar to a Bronte or Dickens heroine (the ones who don't die). I wanted to have an expat flat near the university; I wanted to be able to speak English every day; I wanted to drink tea, gin and tonic, go to Noel Coward plays, shop at places like Harrods. But my real life was anything but. Sayers, writing in the 30s and 40s, would never have imagined that her Wimsey books would become the beginning of someone's life-long love in far-off Hong Kong several decades later.

Pasternak at the U.S. Information Centre

In the 60s, there were three places where one could borrow or read English books without belonging to Hong Kong University: the City Hall library, the British Council Reading Room, and the U.S. Information Centre. The last was housed in a two-storey building on Ice House Street. Even though I walked up and down Ice House Street in 2005, I could not quite pinpoint where the building would have been back in the 60s. I believe the Information Centre is now incorporated into the U.S. Consulate on Garden Road. And judging by the security and long queues, I doubt if anyone could just stroll in and pick a book off the shelf to read. But that was what I did regularly in the late 60s, perhaps as an escape from my father's bedridden presence in the flat, and later, to continue some kind of intellectual activities though I was no longer in school. But in those days of global innocence, anyone could walk into the U.S. Information Centre. Undoubtedly there were cameras; but there was no coded entry, no alarm system. (I walked by the same kind of institution in Berlin, near the Zoo Bahnhof. Not only was the building barricaded; soldiers with weapons patrolled the perimeters.)

I had only used the ground floor. It was a big room serving as a library. Most of the books were by American writers. But I also found it had a good section on Russian literature and history.

Dr. Zhivago, the David Lean film, was first shown in Hong Kong in 1966. I fell in love with it. Not with Omar Sharif, who played Zhivago with dog-brown tear-filled eyes. Not with Tom Courtney, who played the stoical Pasha Antipov. I was entranced by the goldenness of Julie Christie's Lara though. But more than anything, I was in love with the story, the sceneries, the whole constructed Russianness of the film. I went to see it ten times, even during my mother's operation and hospitalization (I forgot what the operation was for.) And because of the film, I read the novel. The first copy of *Dr. Zhivago* I owned was published in conjunction with the opening of the film in 1966. The front cover shows Sharif's Zhivago saying goodbye to Lara in Varykino. The back cover shows the golden profile of Christie, glowering and smouldering in a dark winter coat. This 1966 copy of *Dr. Z* travelled the same route as the Sayers titles. I have bought a hardcover version since, because the paperback was falling apart, being held together by layers of tape. But I still use the tattered copy.

My love for *Dr. Z* extended to the writer, Boris Pasternak. I read everything written by him that was available in translation: *Safe Conduct*, his autobiography and short stories; *Last Summer*, his novella; his letters to his Georgian friends in the 30s; and biographies of the writer. I think the U.S. Information Centre collected Pasternak because he was viewed as an enemy of the Soviet State. One of the books I read was a collection of his poetry, with the Cyrillic original on the facing page. I painstakingly copied the Russian original, even though I didn't know a single alphabet of Russian. I wonder what anyone observing the readers' activities would make of this? Whatever the surveillance people might have thought, this intense self-immersion in Pasternak and Russian must have kick-started my passion for non-English literature and led to my studying German, then eventually taking a doctoral degree in Comparative Literature.

Kitchen Sink Brit Lit in the British Council Reading Room

On the second floor of an Art Nouveau building with elegant hanging lamps and black and white marble floor, the British Council Reading Room was what booklovers would imagine to be a little world of cultured Great Britain in the middle of the finance district of Hong Kong. The room was lined with floor-to-ceiling bookshelves, wood refectory tables, and classroom chairs. It was a general oasis of calm and learning. The building is gone now (Gloucester Building), replaced by a glass and steel version. And when I visited the new British Council in 2006, there was no Reading Room, and the users of the institution were mainly students hoping to get admission to some English universities.

It is ironic, in retrospect, that I should discover not the high culture of Matthew Arnold but the Kitchen Sink genre of British literature in the 60s: *A Taste of Honey, The Loneliness of the Long Distance Runner, Saturday Night and Sunday Morning, Room at the Top* … I read indiscriminately. I didn't really have any guidance once I left Maryknoll, and honestly, I don't think those nuns were up-to-date readers of contemporary literature. I was also goaded into read Joyce's *Ulysses* in the Reading Room. It came about like this. I went to see the filmed version without knowing anything about James Joyce. Naturally, I was confused and somewhat bored (I was only in my late teens.) Taking a book out — probably a Hardy — I happened to mention to the library assistant, a Chinese with a British accent, that I saw the film *Ulysses* but didn't really like it. I believe I was trying to impress him since I envied his accent and his job. He was so obviously superior to me, having the opportunity to live with books and to work for the Brits. He had a little smile on his face as he listened to me, then asked, "But have you read the book?" I was stung and almost the next day, began reading Joyce.

But the Kitchen Sink novels made a stronger impression on me. Or maybe the films adapted from the Kitchen Sink novels impressed me so much that I began to read the originals. Who can forget a young Rita Tushingham in black-and-white despair because she is pregnant and the only consoling friend she has is a whey-faced actor whom I later recognized in *Barry Lyndon*? The film *A Taste of Honey* and the drab filmed reality of working-class England acquired some immeasurable glamour in my eyes. Others' misery could be one's exotic entertainment. Or the brooding handsome face of Laurence Harvey in *A Room at the Top*, with his brilliantined hair and tightly knotted tie and his equally tight voice? Or the impossibly beautiful Terence Stamp in *Poor Cow*, bedding some woman in a miniskirt and pale pink lips. This is the flipside of Sayers's aristocratic world of Lord Peter and duchesses and limitless bank accounts. And I loved both worlds without preference — both worlds were English, part of the colonial culture that I grew up in, exotic and emotionally and/or sexually liberated. People had conversations. Spoke their minds. Fought with a kind of logic that I could understand. More than anything, they provided me with an escape from the Chinese world of Hong Kong, the world I was destined to live in, much to my despair.

Hotels and Hospitals

What kind of future did I have after Maryknoll? My father was certain that I should go into banking, as all the Ngs seemed to have done; all resulting in financial successes, except my father, who remained an employee of a smallish bank until his death. No doubt I could have had a lucrative career in banking if I had wanted, given the contacts my father's extended family could provide. But that profession didn't attract me. Instead, I wanted to go into nursing. Actually, my first choice was to become a foreign correspondent in Vietnam. The perceived excitement of the job, the idea of travelling and being away from my mother, and to write — they were alluring. But my mother wouldn't even consider it remotely, so I applied to Queen Mary Hospital for its training course. (Sad that it would not have occurred to my mother or me that I could have studied medicine. A matter of economic reality as well as gender stereotype.) And now, after spending a happy decade studying for my several degrees, I could understand my choice back then. I wanted to keep on studying, but obviously we didn't have the money to send me to Hong Kong University, which was not a subsidized post-secondary institution the way Canadian universities are. Studying nursing, though not exactly studying literature, was at least a form of post-secondary education. But while I was waiting to hear if I got accepted by Queen Mary Hospital's nursing school, I needed to find some kind of employment to fill in the months of inactivity.

On the other side of travelling

Hotels, no matter how posh, do not intimidate me, because I had stood for nearly a year behind the reception desk of one of the top hotels in Hong Kong. (It's still an expensive place, though given Hong Kong's glut of five-stars hotels, it is no longer all that special. In 1993, I stayed in one of its three towers and vastly enjoyed being on the paying side of the reception desk.)

Like newsreaders on television, hotel receptionists are visible to hotel guests only from the waist up. I used to wear an orange uniform with cream trimming. It was a sleeveless mini-dress with a drop-waist and pleated skirt. Nothing could have made me look worse. The colour was wrong; the style was wrong. As with all uniforms, they only look good on people with model figures. My male colleagues wore a blue — not navy but thankfully, not pale — blazer with black pants. When we worked together behind the cream marble counter and in front of the burl wood wall of mail slots, we were a colourful lot.

I believe I was the most educated of the front desk staff, in that I came from a bilingual private school and actually spoke fairly fluent and unaccented English. I could have lengthy conversations with the international guests and I even had the right body language. Often Chinese, who were shy or wary of mixing with Europeans or North Americans, would display a body language indicating reserve, almost a turning-away from these foreigners. They weren't subservient per se; they were uninterested. My colleagues who didn't speak English competently usually would behave very quietly. Some would cross their arms defensively while speaking to guests, as if protecting themselves from the invasion of the Westerners. In contrast, my good friend and a fellow receptionist, a Eurasian young woman, and I would accost guests who were friendly, chatted to them, joked with them, and even flirted with the men.

One of the more colourful men who worked with us came from Vietnam. He spoke Cantonese, French, and Japanese fluently, but his English was terrible. We usually had to bail him out when he was dealing with English-speaking guests. My girl friend and I liked him because he was funny, had an attitude, spoke his mind, was totally uninterested in the petty power struggles that dominated the many dead hours in the hotel. In the summer months, when he and I worked the night shift that ended at midnight, a group of us would taxi to Sha Tin in the New Territories, virtually the countryside in the early 70s, to have chicken congee. I don't think the congee was better in Sha Tin than in Kowloon, but it was a mini-journey, and Hong Kong people, so confined in everyday life, always sought out ways to have an adventure — a drive to Repulse Bay, a trip to a village in the New Territories for lunch. My parents did that when I was a child. And my relatives still, in 2005, when several of us took a rather circuitous route to a small but densely populated town in New Territories, because a restaurant (more a hole in the wall) there was known for its barbecued goose.

By the time the hotel crew got back to Tsim Sha Tsui, the Star Ferry that connected Kowloon to Hong Kong had stopped. To get across to the Hong Kong side, I needed to take one of those privately run walla wallas. Then a minicab to Causeway Bay. Usually I would be home by about three in the morning. I was only eighteen then, but my mother, with her naïveté regarding the hotel business and work in general, thought that I was working for a prestigious employer and would, therefore, be safe, while she panicked when I didn't come home till 2 am as a university student in Canada.

(I always thought it was ironic that Asian hotels usually get voted hotels with the best service in posh travel magazines. Of course these Thai or Hong Kong or Mumbai hotels could provide excellent service, given that the hotels could afford a high guest-server ratio because of the low wages.)

When I was a front-desk clerk in the 70s, there were always three or four of us for each shift, and all we had to do was to answer questions, hand out room keys, book restaurants, and be generally pleasant. We didn't even have to check people into the hotel — we had reservation clerks to take care of that. Understandably, we spent a lot of time chatting, joking, gossiping, and fighting during each shift. It wasn't a particularly challenging job, but it was fun and I learned how to deal with gweilos and their female counterparts, the gweipos. (I "met" Neville Marriner, who was a very polite man. He and the Academy of St. Martin in the Fields stayed at the hotel. I also caught a glimpse of Germaine Greer and had to deny her existence to people who came to the front desk asking for her room number.)

The front desk manager was a Eurasian of Egyptian or Middle-Eastern ethnicity. His secretary — rumours had it that she was actually a spy for the general manager of the hotel — was a British woman with impeccable dress sense. She never spoke to us, but would smile politely in an aloof way. She had an upper-class accent (or maybe all Brits had an upper-class accent to me then); and she had an upper-class name. She wore dresses that were fashionably tailored and stilettos. The women were in awe of her. While she was glamorous to me then, in retrospect, she probably was very much in the mould of the colonial memsahib — stern, with a sense of entitlement, well but not fashionably dressed, someone from a Le Carré novel. The senior management — five managers — were all Swiss except one. He was ethnic Chinese but I doubted if he even spoke any of the dialects. The hotel was in effect a microcosm of the ethnic and power hierarchy of Hong Kong the city: the Europeans dominating the Chinese by virtue of their social positions, while the Chinese hit back by banding together and supporting each other, speaking in Cantonese to erect a linguistic fence against their foreign supervisors. It was quite usual that the minute one of the managers turned his back, someone would make the most scurrilous and insulting remarks in Cantonese, a rebellious and racialized gesture to even the social ledger.

I believe that, because the exchanges between guests and clerks were so routine (how to get to the Star Ferry, how far is it to the Peak etc.), some of my colleagues got by with rudimentary English. It must be also the reason why I got to know some of the hotel guests better than my colleagues, because I could talk to them beyond the formulaic exchanges. One was a charming redheaded boy from New Zealand. He was staying at the hotel with his family, and usually we would chat after their day's outing — where they went, what they saw, or what Christ Church was like. They stayed for maybe a week. On the day of their departure, the little boy came to the front desk and gave me a box of perfumed soaps. I carried the soaps with me from Hong Kong to Vancouver, and it was only a few years ago that I decided to use them, because they were losing their fragrance. I thought it was a very romantic gesture, even though it was that of a boy of no more than six or seven.

Another "suitor" was not a guest, but his mother was. He had a double-barrel name and even then, not familiar with the social world of England, I knew it was an upper-class name. She stayed at the hotel for months, instead of staying with her son. I didn't know what his profession was, but his flat was in the Mid-Levels area, where non-Chinese and wealthy Chinese lived. It was a low-rise walk-up — a sure indication that the inhabitant had money, since few apartments in Hong Kong were low-rises because of the population and the lack of land. I got to know where he lived because he tried to take me back to his apartment after a movie date. We went to see a sappy film called *Friends*, with a soundtrack featuring Elton John songs. I was eighteen and, though it was fine going to see a film with a man, it wasn't acceptable to visit some man's flat at midnight. I still remember his frustration when I refused to get out of the car — it was a farcical scene, really. He drove a Beetle, and we were crammed inside this little car, because it was winter and we had coats on. He was a tall, gaunt man (at least fifteen years older than me), and he had his arm around my shoulder, trying to convince me that I should get out of the car. "I even bought cakes," he reasoned, and even then, in my naïveté, I thought it was hardly persuasive. I didn't get out of the car. He had to drive me back to Causeway Bay, and after a few more fruitless telephone calls, he gave up pursuing me.

I enjoyed his attention and must have given him reasons to presume that we could become more intimate than just going out to see a film. I realized later that I was what was rudely called a cock-teaser. But it was flattering to be dated by European men — they usually had money, and they had the kind of sophistication that local boys couldn't compete with. And the hotel guests were travellers — they represented to me the world outside, overseas, exotic places, cultures that condoned women sleeping with men if they wanted to, cultures that enjoyed literature, cultures that promoted higher education and all the other values that were absent in my Hong Kong. It was no wonder that I wanted these — generally sexually oriented — invitations; but mindful of my upbringing and the inevitable cataclysmic reaction of my mother, I also stopped short of actually sleeping with anyone.

These early and rather gauche encounters with Western men weren't just adventures of a young and naïve Chinese woman. They inevitably acculturated me to the company of Westerners, especially men, much to my family's discomfort, and my mother's dismay. The most bizarre incident occurred when I was taken to Jimmy's Kitchen to lunch by an old Spaniard who claimed that he was a famous writer. Jimmy's Kitchen — one in Tsim Sha Tsui and one in Central — were expensive restaurants decorated in an old European style. The owners were rumoured to be wealthy Russians who fled the revolution and came to Hong Kong via Shanghai. The interior was predominantly red-velvet wallpaper and plush seats. The waiters wore long white aprons and bowties. Jimmy's Kitchen was famous for its borscht and mixed grill. Since I couldn't afford to go there myself and my mother didn't have the sophistication to take me there, I jumped at the invitation. Because he was old I thought I would be safe. But he spent the whole lunch with his free hand either on my back or my breast. (He was most groping during the Rum Baba and I was really annoyed, because it wasn't often that I had such interesting food to eat. To this day, I have a distinct aversion towards any so-called "old world European" style and "old European masculine charm" — it's creepily mouldy.)

Not every non-Chinese man who took me out was so ungentlemanly. A businessman from Cologne took me twice to dinner, before and after he went to Guangzhou's trade fair. He never assaulted me, and gave me huge bottles of Mitsuoko by Guerlain, which I still like for sentimental reasons. Those were the encounters I truly enjoyed, because it was not threatening and, at the same time, I got a taste of what a European social world was like. This German told me about the cities, about the weathers, about the wines in Europe, and encouraged me to travel. Through these dates, I practised conversing to Westerners socially, instead of the routine answers required in the job. I suppose these men were a series of Professors Higgins.

It was not an easy time to grow up bi-culturally. It was the decade of sexual liberation, of the Beatles, of mini-skirts. I had access to all the news and trends through television, magazines, films. Unlike my more Chinese-centric friends, I wanted to be liberated. But there were so many ramifications.

If I should sleep with a European without marrying him, I would be considered no better than a whore. But I could never marry a European, given my very Chinese background. My mother wouldn't even entertain the faintest possibility of its happening. Furthermore, where could I sleep with any of these men? Certainly not in a hotel — the very idea seemed tawdry to me. ("Tawdry" would be the kind of words I would use, picking it up from reading British novels.) I didn't have a flat of my own, and I knew no one who had a flat of her own. So, while I wanted to behave very much like one of the liberated women wearing a Mary Quant mini-skirt and smoking Gaulois (*Blow-Up* or *Darling* came to mind), I remained a timid and virtuous virgin who flirted. (In 2005, I didn't see many couples of mixed ethnicities in Hong Kong except in bars, though they are a common sight in Vancouver.)

One hotel guest I got to know did have his own place. He would be the first American man I befriended, in an odd sort of way. He was staying at the hotel with his girlfriend. She was one of the liberated types I yearned to be. She had Julie Christie hair, wore hoop earrings, very short skirts, and white boots. She was tall, had a wide mouth with full lips and milk-white skin that Chinese young women envied. I thought she was gorgeous. Her lover liked talking to me and eventually, when he got his own place, invited me to visit them. This encounter taught me that, even though people could communicate linguistically, the secrets and shades of cultural practices could remain totally inaccessible. Since this American and his lover talked to me often at the hotel, I presumed that my spoken English was quite fluent and that I would be able to access their social world. Yet, my two visits to his place completely baffled me, as if I was socializing with someone who suddenly spoke a different language and behaved differently.

He rented a whole house that was set in its own garden. It was near Blue Pool Road, not far from Maryknoll and other places where my schoolmates lived. It was one of the older buildings in Hong Kong that no longer exists today. Built for rich Hong Kongers or colonial administrators, it was of stone and resembled an English country house, but on a smaller scale, with a driveway and iron fences. The front hall had fireplaces and a very high ceiling. It had three storeys and I don't know why the couple needed such a large place, even though they had a Great Dane.

Since this American had a girlfriend living with him, I thought it would be perfectly fine to accept his invitation. I was curious and I wanted to show off to my girlfriends. We talked — I mostly told him how depressed I found my future in Hong Kong to be; how I longed to travel and live somewhere else; how I thought Camus and D.H. Lawrence were great writers — mainly I talked like a well-read teenager, a geek. He listened sometimes, and he laughed at me at other times. The first time I visited, he took me up a rather grand staircase to the second floor, where his bedroom was. He said his girlfriend was around the house somewhere. There was no bed, just a mattress on the floor. I suspect now that they rented the place partly furnished, for whatever purpose. We sat on one end of mattress and talked; it didn't occur to me that being in a bedroom with a man alone had certain significations. It showed that acquiring knowledge through reading and through experience are quite distinct. To add to this surreal scene (to me), I could hear his girlfriend roaming around the house with the Great Dane. Nothing happened between us — a running discourse on literature couldn't be very seductive. Finally, his girlfriend called him on the house phone and our session came to an end. He was polite enough to invite me back, even though he must have thought that I had wasted his time. (Could he have been a psychoanalyst? That might explain his willingness to listen to me …)

I did go back one more time. I couldn't resist — their lifestyle, the house, the dog, the alcohol that seemed part of their diet — I would have loved to live like that. I didn't really worry if my presence in the very same house with his girlfriend was anomalous. I thought that was the way relationships were conducted in European and American countries. Somehow, in a totally muddled way, I thought it was very D.H. Lawrence. Of course it was nothing like that. Whatever his profession was, this American lived in an egocentric world and he enjoyed indulging himself, be it food, wine, women, or marijuana, which he offered me to try. I suppose now I would call him some wealthy hippie in the 70s spending some time in the so-called Orient, taking advantage of what the locals could offer. He had an assistant or secretary who was Chinese. He looked a bit like John Lone — very suave, very tailored, very smooth. When I was leaving after a more pointless and puzzling second visit, the American said to his assistant who had just arrived, "She is the most depressed girl I have ever met!" His assistant, who was seeing me to the front gate, smirked but said nothing. I didn't quite understand what was going on but I did feel that my presence was a mistake, that I had nothing in common with these sophisticated people from the United States, who ate steaks and drank wine and slept on the floor and left underpants lying around.

It was my first introduction to that mysterious condition that one experiences when one is plunged into a strange culture, even though one believes that there is no language barrier. Immigrants experience this condition constantly. You read the menu; you can order the food; you are dressed the same as the other diners; but when the food arrives, you realize that first, you don't like the taste, and second, you don't even know the proper way to eat it. This is a mundane example of the disconnect that dominates intercultural experiences.

Decades later I studied Postcolonialism and read Edward Said and other critics writing on orientalist practices, and these days while I was working at the hotel came into focus and acquired a context. Though I was not a glamorous-looking young woman, I was young and somewhat naïve and perfectly willing to entertain these *gweilos*, albeit non-sexually. In a way, I was acquiring cultural knowledge by talking to them and eating with them. I suppose that they were hoping for something more. If nothing else, they had the brief experience of going out with an "oriental" woman.

A nurse is like a housemaid in a hotel

If the hotel introduced me to men with orientalist attitudes, the Queen Mary Hospital took me back to a life of discipline, schedules, sheer hard work. The process of becoming a nurse in the early 70s involved a regular rotation between practicum and theory. We spent three months studying, then three months in a ward. We lived in the dormitory, shared rooms, and ate in the refectory. My first week as a student nurse was hell, because I had never lived with strangers (I had two roommates), never shared bathrooms with strangers, and after the rather luxurious world of the hotel, even though I was only part of the serving crew, the austerity of the hospital dormitory was shocking. There were rules about everything, from when to turn the lights off to when we could send our nursing uniforms to the laundry.

A morning shift in the wards began at 6.30, which meant getting up at 5.30. On many tropical dawns while the patients were still sleeping, I would be walking around the beds gathering sputum mugs and taking pulse rates, before I even had breakfast. When it became gradually light, I would be standing in the little instrument room, measuring the quantity of a patient's sputum and writing down its appearance. One of these rooms had a big window that opened out to the Pacific Ocean, since the Queen Mary Hospital stood on the hill and was not far from the water. It wouldn't be the Pacific Ocean exactly, but the water would lead to it, and as I was writing down the appearance of the greenish sputum of bed 5, I looked out the window and thought about the unknown world that existed beyond the sheet of water shimmering in the morning light. I wanted desperately to become part of that world, to get away from the hospital, away from the Chinese, from steamed rice, and from my mother. I wanted freedom and, somehow, I saw it through that window every morning when I worked the morning shift. (While looking at the view — the blue water and the blue sky, the islands dotted around the coastline — I always hummed Dvorak's *New World Symphony* as I was performing my chores.)

Breakfast was at 7.30, after we had done the initial round of the ward. We walked back to our dormitory and hurried through congee or noodles in the dining hall. There would be over a hundred nurses — the students in pink and the graduated nurses in blue — talking and eating. The noise was deafening and it reminded me of Sayers's *Gaudy Night*. I gradually got to like this camaraderie. Then back to the ward. We made beds, changed bedpans, checked drips, washed wounds, and followed the house doctor around, behind the matron and the staff nurse. At ten, it was teatime and a much-anticipated break — bread and butter, jam and tea and milk. Someone might suggest everyone chipping in to buy some chocolate digestives. (How incongruous it was that the hospital breakfast was strictly Chinese but our tea was always very English.) The morning shift got off at 1.30 for lunch and the rest of the day was free. I don't remember what the afternoon shift was like and student nurses never had to work the night shift.

I adored the matron who taught us. She was tall and slender and had reddish hair. She was Scottish and had the most charming accent. Her skin was milky pale and without blemish. She was also tough — totally without sentiment. But she was a good teacher.

We had to deal with another matron who left me an indelible impression that she was a man masquerading as a woman. She was wide and stocky, and for some reason, she wore bright red lipstick that gave her the appearance of being wounded, because she also had fair skin, which became mottled when she was upset. She wasn't soft-spoken and used to shout her commands like someone in an army would. Actually, I thought she was both like a man and a soldier. Even the doctors feared her, because she was senior and she was rough. My fellow students had problems dealing with the matrons because many of them had no experience of non-Chinese teachers. But for me, it was an extension of the years studying with the nuns. (It didn't seem odd to me then that all the student nurses were Chinese. Obviously, the idea that a Westerner might be changing the bedpan of some Chinese patient would be too bizarre. Such was the kind of racial assumptions that became quite acceptable in a colonial culture.)

The doctors were always a delight. They were heroes if they were senior house doctors or specialists. And they were potential husbands if they were young and single. I wasn't interested in marrying a doctor — I think I was interested in a poet or a writer then. I didn't have the looks anyway to compete with some of my colleagues. Some of them were really stunning, and of course we snidely remarked that they only became student nurses because they were husband-hunting. Still, there must be easier ways to look for a husband than through a job that required changing dressing at 6.30 in the morning. But I admired the doctors because they were trained professionals. Unlike those characters I worked with at the hotel, some of whom were virtual illiterates. At that time, I realized that a recognized profession, such as the medical, could confer dignity on the person, no matter how ugly, short, and Chinese that person might be. (This notion was vindicated when I read Pierre Bourdieu's *Distinction* at university.)

One of our favourite pastimes — amongst the few student nurses who became a clique — was to stay up and watch the doctors returning to their dorms after a night shift, usually at midnight. Since we were still somewhat immature — we were all in our late teens — we would drape ourselves in sheets and made ghostly noises as individual doctors walked by. The student dormitory was one of the older buildings on the hill. It had stone pillars and balconies that looked out — at that time — to the sea. Those of us not working the afternoon shift would spend our summer evenings sitting on the balconies in cane furniture, enjoying the sunset as we recycled the day's gossip, made plans for the weekend, or exchanged lecture notes. Gradually, I came to embrace this communal lifestyle. I liked the discipline — it was a challenge but I also needed it. I didn't mind the long hours working on my feet — we had to wear padded shoes for comfort and supporting hosiery for our legs! I spent a lot of time washing my hands and I could always smell the ward, the patients, the sickness on my uniform. But I thought being a nurse was a worthwhile way to spend my time. But not my whole life.

That year I spent studying nursing was, in a way, a continuation of my life at Maryknoll. Uniform. Discipline. Lectures and exams. Friends. Summer days. Walks in a relatively pleasant environment that resembled the countryside, even though the city was really down the hill and a short bus ride away. And quite consciously, I was glad that I lived a life that was totally closed to my mother's influence, even though I had to call her regularly. Studying nursing was also a way to spend my time that she could not criticize because of its obvious respectability. I did well in the theoretical parts of the training, passing exams with good grades, though my class demonstrations could have been more professional. (I tended to giggle when I dressed a pretend wound on the gardener's head.) There would be no doubt that I would graduate. (When I told the head instructor that I was leaving the programme, he said that I would have been one of the top graduates, but of course, if I had the chance to attend university in Canada, the choice was clear.)

The immigration papers arrived. We were going to Canada.

A Week in My Life (Before I Left Hong Kong Forever!)

Between Maryknoll Sisters School and the university, I worked every week. Except for the few months before we immigrated to Canada. I learned the hospitality business and I learned about the hospital culture. I learned that I enjoyed working; that I could adapt to different social environments; and that between Maryknoll culture and my Chinese parents' influence, I had developed a scrupulous attitude towards earning a living.

I was never late and often stayed beyond the time to leave my shift. I observed rules and followed them. I realized that people often couldn't get along with each other in close proximity and that, unless one was the boss, one would have to compromise. (My mother never really worked and hence, she didn't understand the concept of compromise, especially in personal relationships.) Intelligence could count for a lot, almost more than good looks. I wasn't good-looking but I was arguably one of the smartest amongst my colleagues, in the hotel or at the hospital. I also realized that people in supervisory positions weren't always qualified. That they could be morons. That they could be corrupt.

Thus, by the time I was getting ready to leave my old life behind and start a new one, I was a very cynical twenty-year-old. I modelled myself on the main character in Sartre's *Nausea* (another book I carried around with me from place to place, country to country, and is falling apart.) I believed that I was a keen observer and often struck a pose in public places, such as coffee shops, looking world-weary and exaggeratedly detached. Unfortunately I didn't have the money to buy a wardrobe to go with the pose. I saw around me people of my own race, who spoke the same language, but who had totally different values and life goals. I didn't want to make lots of money (though aware that I would have a better time with money than without.) I wanted to read poetry and discuss literature with like-minded friends. I couldn't abide by the pure commercialism of Hong Kong society. I really was ready to begin a new life, with a new identity, with new habits, with new thoughts.

I was ready to leave behind all my friends, whether from school, from the hotel, or from the nursing school. I don't think I took a single Hong Kong address with me. If I did, I certainly don't have the contact now.

We got some money from selling the apartment. I still don't know if my father left any assets other than the apartment and maybe his pension. My mother was very secretive about financial arrangements, her mantra being, "We'll manage." But we agreed that I should quit studying nursing as soon as we got the go-ahead from the Canadian government. And those few months of waiting were rather blissful ones as a watershed between languishing in a city that I was tiring of and a future of which I could not yet imagine.

I had some money saved from work. My mother also gave me a small allowance. With modest means, I lived for the first time a carefree life, a sort of low-grade tai-tai life. Tai-tai is a gendered class concept in Hong Kong. It approximates the-ladies-who-lunch. A tai-tai has limitless money to lunch at the Mandarin Oriental or the Four Seasons. She is chauffeured around in a Rolls Royce or a Mercedes. She wears Chanel suits or Versace couture, and she is recognized as a good client in the luxury shopping complexes such as the Landmark. She has her hair styled regularly in a salon. Her husband is some captain of industry, who takes her out, adorned in Cartier diamonds, to social events that get featured in the Hong Kong versions of *Hello* magazine or *US*. I thought that the tai-tai would have been slowly phased out, with China taking over Hong Kong and with feminism. But in 2005, as I was walking out of the Central Building onto Pedder Street, I stood aside and watched a tai-tai in her forties getting out of her Mercedes, supported by her maid in the classic servant uniform of a Chinese white top and black loose pants. Her other staff cleared a path for her to walk into the building, where Louis Vuitton and other luxury brands had retail outlets. I shook my head in disbelief.

Our routine was nothing like that, of course. But my mother and I lunched out every day at the same restaurant — a medium-priced but well known Chinese restaurant on Des Voeux Road, just before the neighbourhood turned into Sheung Wan. A seat was reserved for us and the servers greeted us as Mrs. Ng and Miss Ng. After lunch we would take the tram to Happy Valley to visit my father's grave. Then we went shopping for suitable clothes to take with us to Canada. We visited my mother's friends to say goodbye. I was quite happy to accompany her because I knew that it would be the last time I had to perform this duty. There were endless farewell dinners hosted by friends and relatives. In the 70s, going abroad was still a novelty for Chinese in Hong Kong. We acquired social status. We were going to live in a house!

Dining out and shopping — the twin obsessions of Hong Kong Chinese, or many Chinese everywhere. In those few liminal months, I thoroughly enjoyed being a regular Hong Konger. I stopped railing against consumerism and philistinism. I gave in to not having a regular schedule. I read and watched television. Went to foreign films and concerts at the City Hall, pretending that I could tell a Walton symphony from a Schumann piece. I was pretentious and the memory still embarrasses me. Maybe that's why now I can't take seriously people who go to operas and concerts regularly and think they are culturally superior.

I was being courted by some man who thought that the way to winning my attention was taking me out and giving me presents. He won my mother's heart because he gave her expensive presents too. But for me, it was another way to spend time before I finally could leave a city that had palled on me. To grab my luggage and get on the plane. I can't remember his name or what he looked like.

I must have seen some of my own friends — but no one stood out in my memory. Not true. One young woman who went to Maryknoll and whose family apartment I visited almost daily for a while — she and I got on rather well even after Maryknoll, and we were both kicking our heels before she also left Hong Kong for Toronto. We spent some time chatting about freedom and individual expressions, about how soulless Hong Kong was, about the wonderful North American culture, about Simon and Garfunkel, about love, and so on. I told her about being dumped by Richard. She told me about being rejected by someone (I suspected it might be one of the nuns). Her rather wealthy family, who used to look askance at my frequent visits when we were both at school, suddenly found that I was a bit more acceptable, because I too was going to live abroad. As a matter of fact, I believed the rather snobbish mother said that her daughter and I should keep in touch in Canada, a thought that would never have crossed her mind if both of us were staying in Hong Kong.

Otherwise, I can remember no one I spent any tearful farewells with. I could not wait to leave. I wish I could say that I felt a tinge of regret. Or that the spring days looked more lovely than ever in Hong Kong. Or that I would miss all the amenities — the variety of restaurants, the many shops, the vibrant city itself. Or that I realized suddenly that I was giving up a future that promised a top job in banking through the Ng connections. Nothing of the sort. Nor did I worry about living in Vancouver, Canada. That I would be speaking in English in order to function socially. Or that I would need to study in a totally different environment. Or that I would have to make new friends.

In my callow youthfulness, I was both fearless and self-centred. I could not imagine what this cutting-off from a familiar and comfortable life would be like for my mother. Or that she would have no language, since Vancouver in the 70s was not so populated with Chinese the way it is today. Or that she would be afraid. My mother was always in charge. She always presumed to know the answers to any situations. To me, she would carry on knowing how to deal with life in Vancouver as she did in Hong Kong. Of course, the reality was very different. But that belongs to another narrative. However, if I had been less anxious to leave Hong Kong, less naïve, I should have known that by leaving Hong Kong with my widowed mother, I was taking on a life-long debt in addition to the edicts of Confucianist filial piety. My mother left Hong Kong for me — I was never allowed to forget that.

Palimpsests

The Waterfront

Both Macau and Hong Kong share the allure of a city on the water and they implanted in my psyche an undiminished need to be near a body of water. Not to swim in or sail in. Just to look at, to know it is there. I cannot imagine living far away from the sea, because it provides ready escape. A medieval concept, since one can fly, if one can't sail.

Hong Kong Island is surrounded by water, but like the peninsula across the harbour, only a small part of it could be negotiated on foot. Or at least, that one would want to. Even in the 60s, when I started to walk the city in my pretentious teenage existential funk, the esplanade, or some version of an esplanade, extended only from Queen's Pier, where one could hire water taxis, westward towards the government piers, where one boarded ferries to Macau or Guangzhou. Altogether about a fifteen-minute walk. Otherwise, the waterfront in Hong Kong, stretching from Kennedy Town (west) to Shau Kei Wan (east) was developed, with shops or warehouses or highrises or the 60s version of freeways. To enjoy a European-style waterfront, with sandy beach, elegant walkways, or like the Ribiera in Porto, with cafés under umbrellas, one had to drive to resorts such as Repulse Bay or Stanley Bay. Repulse Bay boasted the colonial hotel of the same name, which was too expensive for us, but we liked having picnics at the Lido with the extended family. Stanley Village had a market, but until the 90s, it wasn't a destination of choice for Chinese.

On the Kowloon side, the waterfront was even more compromised. Along Salisbury Road was the railway track that led to China. Further north were densely populated neighbourhoods such as Hung Hom and To Kwa Wan, where my cousin now lives. On the west side of the peninsula were piers for P&O and Cunard liners, as well as freighters. Then swathes of industrial land, warehouses, factories, then villages as it got closer to the New Territories. These were areas I knew very little about. Hong Kong physically is a small place, but in terms of the complexities of its urban geography, it rivals much bigger cities such as Berlin or New York, though it does not have the long history of a London or a Paris.

The only area I could walk that was close to the water on Kowloon side was the peninsula tip where the Star Ferry was. And of course, the Star Ferry, a five-minute ride across the harbour, was itself a water-front experience.

In 1993, I stayed for a month in the hotel where I used to work. Actually, I stayed in its sister hotel, another highrise next door. I arrived close to midnight. After dropping off my bags and looking in dismay at the sealed-in room, I took the elevator down to the second floor, where the three hotels were linked by a shopping mall. I might have to walk down to Canton Road, but after ten minutes of wandering, I got out next to the Ocean Terminal, a mecca for Sunday outings for my father, my mother, and myself. Then I caught one of the last ferries across the harbour. It was December but it was warm. I smelled diesel. I saw palm trees. I saw uncountable lights on buildings. I saw water as black as tar. Sitting on the bench of seats that had movable backrests, I watched the mirage of the black silhouette that was the Victoria Peak growing larger and thought to myself, "I am home." I never regret leaving Hong Kong, but a few things remain affectionately vivid in my memories — the weather, the sudden downpour, my school, Star Ferry. If the Star Ferry were ever abolished and replaced by another tunnel, in addition to the three or four that already exist, I am not sure I would still feel that strong tie to the city. Much as I can accept that a city changes with time and social necessities, the Star Ferry in Hong Kong is as immutable an urban institution as the Eiffel Tower in Paris or the black cabs in London.

Street Scenes

Although Porto reminds me of Macau overall, because of the Portuguese culture, Porto's hillside streets teeming with little shabby shops resemble a part of Hong Kong that I knew well. As a child and later as a student nurse, I frequently visited the stalls on Pottinger Street and Ladder Street. To get from the waterfront area to the hillside neighbourhoods — University of Hong Kong, Roman Catholic cathedral, Sacred Heart Girl School — the buses trundle along two main streets that intersect a series of alleys and lanes that cascade down what historically was the hillside but now are fully developed real estate properties. Hollywood Road is the lower, or northerly road skirting around the old Victoria Prison. Caine Road is the upper conduit that takes the traveller from the leafy environs of the Botanical Gardens and the former Government

House to the less leafy but equally prestigious environs of Hong Kong University. In between are streets with quaint names that bear witness to the colonial ghettoization in that area — Chancery Lane, Old Bailey Street, Elgin Street, Cochrane Street, Gutzlaff Street, Peel Street ... Then suddenly, it's Shin Wong Street, Wing Lee Street, as if the Westerners had resided within a territory of twelve intersecting streets and would go no further.

Some of these streets are very steep and murderous in the summer months. The wealthy that lived there didn't have to negotiate these climbs with their groceries in hand. They had servants to do it. I shuddered to think that rickshaw drivers used to climb up these hills with their passengers. I seem to remember that my mother and I actually rode rickshaw up these slopes to visit some of her friends. Now, a visitor can find a rickshaw on display near the Star Ferry terminal for tourists but not as part of the transportation system. We were so much more inhumane in the past.

Some of the streets are mainly residential — three-storey walk-ups with whitewashed walls and shutters, a hint of the elegant colonial apartments fifty or sixty years ago. Some, like Pottinger and Ladder, are lined with stalls selling anything from ribbons to food. As a student nurse, I and other student nurses on day shift would take the bus and get off at the junction of Hollywood Road and Lyndhurst Terrace, then walk down Ladder Street where the food stalls were crowded with people getting off work or like us, people coming out for a night snack. Noodles with fish balls, barbecued pork on rice, congee, gailan lightly boiled and served in oyster sauce. We took a table teetering on the sloppy sidewalk and slurped our noodles as we recounted the day's adventures in Ward B or the crazy lecture on duodenal ulcer in the morning. The evenings were warm and the street lamps were the main lighting — in memory those outings had a magical sheen that only Wong Kar-wai manages to capture in the Maggie Cheung scenes in *In the Mood for Love*.

I didn't go to Ladder Street during my latest visit, but I walked up and down Elgin, Old Bailey, Pottinger, Ezra, had lunch with a colleague on Shelley Street at the Peak Café; I spent most mornings in an internet café on Hollywood Road, checking email, sipping the first Americano, watching people hurrying off to work, to shop, to life. A wonderful area of compressed urban excitement, of surprising charm, of corners of shaded tranquillity. On a corner of Peel and Hollywood, I was fascinated by a little store that sold shabby household items. The building had three floors above the shop. The windows had green shutters. The outside wall was painted a buttery yellow. The front of the house showed wrought-iron balconies, behind which were levered doors with wooden shutters. It was sadly elegant. It was also architecturally more eloquent than any number of the newly constructed highrises around the area. For example, my colleague rented a little apartment in Soho, in a modern but mean building with no poetry and no streetscape to speak of.

Mornings in big cities are the best time of the whole day. There is something very poignant and tender about the tranquillity of streets that would normally be throbbing with energy and noise; or the emptiness of a plaza devoid of loiterers and ice-cream lickers; or sidewalks free of bistro tables and demitasses. My favourite moments in Porto were the mornings when it was still cool. Amsterdam is at its most seductive at six on a summer morning, when the sparkle from the canal bounces off onto the leaves of the plane trees, when all the cars are at rest instead of struggling along the narrow lanes, when just a whiff of good coffee could be smelled as neighbourhood coffee shops begin the day's work. Or Paris. Or London. Or Berlin.

Hong Kong is no different. Visitors should get up at about 5.30 and start walking the streets. From a practical point of view, it's cooler. And there will be fewer people around. I seemed to have always gotten up really early. School assembly was at 8, so I must have been up before 7 in order to be at school on time by bus. Early hotel shift started at 8 as well. And early shift at the hospital started at 6 or 6.30. Somewhere in my memory bank, I have a picture of myself at eighteen, sullen from some domestic set-to, reading hand-copied notes of Sartre's *Being and Nothingness* on a bench in Edinburgh Place before catching a ferry to cross the harbour to start my shift at the hotel. It could have been an afternoon shift, but I prefer the possibility that I was sitting there at 7.30, catching a few existential paragraphs before joining the hotel world. My favourite morning views, as mentioned before, were from the instruments room in the hospital ward. I didn't know Wordsworth's "Composed Upon Westminster Bridge" then, but the line "The beauty of the morning; silent, bare" would be apt for those few cool, blue moments, when the future was a stretch of water away.

Food

Always important in any version of Chinese culture — Hong Kong Chinese, mainland Chinese, Taiwanese Chinese, Southeast Asian Chinese, Vancouver Chinese ... Let's start with breakfast. I remember some Canadian I met when I first arrived in Vancouver asking me what my family ate for breakfast and I was at a loss for reply. Chinese don't eat cereal and they don't like dairy products much. (They could be acculturated but cheese and yogurt are not part of the diet normally.) Thinking back, I know I was embarrassed that I didn't know what a Canadian breakfast would consist of, as if I was caught cheating. Cheating in being a Canadian. I mumbled something about sandwiches. With more travel experience now, I know that cultures eat different things at different times of the day and there was nothing to be ashamed of because Chinese didn't spoon down cereal with milk at 8 am.

In Hong Kong, I like getting my steaming congee at some unpretentious eatery near where I am staying, something I can't readily get in Canada unless I want to drive to Chinatown. When we had maids, we might have our home-made congee; but I had gone out in the morning when we were living in Causeway Bay, walked to the market stalls on Russell Street, approximately where Times Square is now, to buy takeout congee. I especially liked the kind with fresh pig's blood pudding with lots of ginger shreds. Alternately, I had walked along Causeway Road to the corner of Haven Road, to the local bakery that sold Portuguese buns, buns with ham or egg, or buns with coconut filling. We drank Lipton's red tea with milk with these buns, as opposed to Chinese tea with the congee. My father being a gourmand, we always had fresh everything. The idea of frozen ingredients and microwaved foods would have appalled him.

(One morning during one of my visits, I walked into a little eatery on Canton Road with a friend to get some congee. The place was packed and we were walking towards a table to share with another patron who was already eating his breakfast. In Hong Kong, it is perfectly in order to share tables in most restaurants, which means that one can't have phobia of sharing intimate space and activities with total strangers, but it also means that one can't have intimate conversations over a cosy meal! As I was intent on securing the remaining two chairs at the table, I heard someone loudly calling my friend's name, which was a surprise, considering that it was his first time in Hong Kong. Amazingly, it was someone he worked with in Vancouver, who was also in Hong Kong and eating breakfast at the same place that morning. Hong Kong can be a very small place in spite of its six million natives plus numerous visitors.)

I found that the traditional ways of eating haven't changed since I left Hong Kong in the 70s. One could still find little specialty shops that would sell snake bladders and snake soup. But there are more varieties, in addition to the traditional restaurants that served dim sum. Like many middle-classed Chinese families, we ate out on weekends. When I was younger, we went to a venerable restaurant called Lok Yu on Li Yuen St West, an alley off Des Voeux Road Central. The main business on that narrow street was stalls that sold clothes, handbags, toys, and small shops that sold tea and food ingredients, such as dried mushrooms. Squeezed in amongst the colourful cheap shirts and plastic handbags was Lok Yu, an unassuming two-storey traditional teahouse, the kind that seems so exotic in films such as *Crouching Tiger, Hidden Dragon*. The tables and chairs were carved rosewood with inlaids; enamel floral spittoons on the floor; waiters wore cloth slippers, white cotton robes or tops and black pants; and tables were hard to come by. My father was a regular because his bank was nearby and he came for lunch sometimes, so we always got a table with our favourite waiter. Otherwise, even wealthy clients got turned away. In 2005, I took my mother to the new Lok Yu, relocated on Stanley Street. It is still furnished like a traditional teahouse; the food is still expensive; but the waiters, already of a second generation from the ones serving us in the 60s, look as if they were playing a part in a play. They don't have that lordly indifference their older colleagues exuded.

We never went to Lok Yu with the extended family — aunts, uncles, grandma etc. It was too expensive for a large group and the restaurant was small. As a large group, we would go to the floating restaurant in Aberdeen as a treat. It has become such a tourist cliché that I don't think I need to dwell on it. It is even featured, in a rather ludicrous scene, in *The World of Suzie Wong*. Replicas of these rather gaudy eating ships can be found even in the West, for example, Amsterdam. I quite liked the floating restaurant concept in Hong Kong — the drive to Aberdeen was an adventure; getting taxied from the pier to the restaurant was always fun; and the scenery was always spectacular. So yes, visitors should have a meal there ...

To know a little-known place where some specialty is served is a sign of sophistication in Hong Kong social circles, high or low. Even those who don't reside in Hong Kong play the game. Recently, I met a friend of my cousin. My cousin works in southern China and lives in Hong Kong on the weekends. Her friend visited Hong Kong regularly but worked in Malaysia. However, after a day trip to the Buddhist shrine on Lantau Island, Teresa's friend suggested that we have dinner at a place in New Territories famous for its barbecued goose. From the peak of Lantau we took a bus down to the town centre of the island, hurdling around some pretty sharp corners on picturesque narrow lanes. From there we took the rapid train to Sheung Kwai Chung, then a taxi to a town that used to be no more than a village, whose name I can't remember. The eatery was about the size of the living room of a large house in Vancouver. I was told not to use the toilet because it was just a hole in the floor. The food was good — we had fresh barbecued goose, steam vegetables, fresh steamed prawns; but at the back of my mind, now so used to North American sanitation, I was wondering how clean everything was. Furthermore, I thought it was an arduous way to get a meal of barbecued goose. But for the Chinese, this was a typical way to socialize.

Shopping

If the Chinese in Hong Kong were not eating, then they would be shopping during leisure time. I was introduced to shopping as a social activity, not just a matter of necessity, at a very young age. As long as I could remember, we always went shopping after lunch on Sundays. (Saturday was not a day-off for my father — most people worked and still work half a day on Saturday). Shopping was a kind of post-prandial exercise. Families bonded over shopping. Social distinctions were established by where one shopped and what one bought. When I was five or six, we would be strolling around the shopping areas downtown. My mother's favourite was Lane Crawford, where I saw my first Mary Quant mini-dress as a teenager, though we couldn't really afford the clothes there. When we lived in Causeway Bay, we went shopping around Lockhart Road and Cannon Street, where a new Japanese department store was opened. Or we would take the Star Ferry across the harbour to Tsim Sha Tsui. I think my parents were more open to Western customs when they were a youngish couple. I remember afternoon teas and cakes in some coffee shop in Prince's Building or Edinburgh Building. I would have been six or seven; my father would be in his forties and my mother thirties. But as my father got older and more ravaged by his cancer, he seemed to have less patience with these non-Chinese practices.

Whenever I went back to Hong Kong, I spent a lot of time looking at the shops. Large and small. During my last visit I bought an Alberta Ferretti skirt and some cosmetics at a new Lane Crawford in Pacific Place, because the original store in Central was torn down. Pacific Place was one of two shopping centres that I, as an exilic Hong Kong Chinese, love for various reasons. The other shopping mall is the IFC Mall.

While staying at a hostel in the Mid-Levels, I walked down Garden Road and turned right at Kennedy Road, passing the once elegant Kennedy Terrace. Some remnants of that elegance still remain in the few two- or three-storey apartment houses in that area. High ceilings, tall windows looking out to the harbour, terraces shaded by palm trees, narrow driveway to the front doors, protecting the houses from the traffic screaming by. Very old money. Some mornings I lingered in front of real estate offices and read notices of the apartments for sale or for rent. In 2005, one could buy a 1,200 square-foot apartment on MacDonnell

Road for HK$7.2 million, or over a million Canadian dollars. Or rent an apartment in the same posh neighbourhood, no larger than 730 square feet, at HK$23,000 a month, or the equivalent of $4,000 in Canada. My cousin's apartment is about a quarter the size of my place in Canada. An expatriate teacher gets a monthly rent allowance of about $1,750 Canadian. To live in decent accommodations in Hong Kong is phenomenally expensive; one's address is as much a social index as it would be in London or Paris.

Continued walking and passed the city villa where the Brits met the Chinese government to cobble together the 1997 takeover. Passed St. Joseph's College and the Visual Arts Centre, another fine example of colonial architecture. (If it were opened, I would walk in for a quick visit.) Several steps down and I was in Hong Kong Park. At ten in the morning, the sun was not as brutal as it would be at noon. The park was not busy and it was a good time to explore the various pathways. When I was living in Hong Kong, this whole area would have been colonial and the only people who had any business there would be Westerners, or government officials. The lower entrance/exit of the park is located on Supreme Court Road. I turned right and reached the British Council, next to the British Consulate. It gave me great pleasure to ride the escalator up to the café, to use its banks of computers, to sit and read the *South China Morning Post*, not as a supplicant or a colonial subject, but as a Canadian who didn't need anything from the institution. Except its free internet service. And its air-conditioning.

After my mid-morning coffee, I took the linking series of escalators and reached the lower level of the Pacific Place, where I had numerous choices for lunch. Also convenient was the food hall, where I could buy Western groceries and take-out dinners. After watching people for a while, I would walk to the stop and wait for the bus that would take me back to the Mid-Levels, along with the school children and the maids out shopping for their employers.

On alternate mornings, I would take a bus downtown. IFC Mall straddles several streets. I liked the route that took me near the Star Ferry terminal. I stopped at an internet café to have coffee and check email messages. Then the bookstore. Or I would stand on the second level of the twin towers, looking down into the atrium of the Central MTR station, where one takes the airport express or goes for early check-in. Sometimes I might stay till late, grabbing a cheap meal at one of the many eateries in IFC mall or one of the other buildings. Looking at late office workers, still checking their computers at seven in the evening. Wondering who the people who sat around the waiting hall of Central MTR were: old men in singlets; women who looked like they might be from Southeast Asia; families. Or imagining that I was home in cold northern Canada, instead of dreading the heat that was waiting outside, even at nine in the evening.

I was several persons at once while visiting the city that had done so much to shape me for over twenty years. I was nostalgic for my happy school days. I was uneasy remembering the family quarrels. I was made aware how Chinese-Cantonese I remained after decades of living in Canada. And I was amused at how I tried to pretend to be somebody else from time to time. All the while, I watched, remembered, compared, reviewed — my past became part of my present.

Maryknoll Sisters School on Blue Pool Road, Hong Kong

A colonial building with terrace
and a typical highrise in Hong Kong

Lan Kwai Fong, Hong Kong

To Write, To Travel

Writing and Travelling

It can be said that I spent the first twenty years of my life — or at least the major part of these twenty years — wanting to be a different person. I didn't want to live in Hong Kong. I didn't like being Chinese. I couldn't imagine myself becoming established and growing old in this city. I couldn't get along with my mother and didn't really want to have much to do with any of the many relatives on both sides of the family. Even good friends disappointed me in that, though they received the same education, read the same books, attended the same lectures, and lived in the same cities, they didn't develop any of these symptoms. Colonial cultures didn't seem to affect them. I was the odd person out.

In reviewing my early life, I try to see my memories from the perspective of this perpetually sullen teenager within the context of the kind of life I led — a constant pattern of conflicting cultural information and an intelligent awareness that outstripped the conventional guidance that was available to me. I think the fictional character I related to most was Paul Morel in D.H. Lawrence's *Sons and Lovers*, although my father was not a violent man of the working class. And although young Morel doesn't want to become an East Asian!

(I can quite see, as an adult, that of course my mother could not explain to me the contradictions in my upbringing. I must be proud of my Chinese heritage; but I must learn to think like a Westerner. I could spend all my time at the convent; but I could not develop any non-Chinese friendship. I could imbibe the ideologies of the Catholic Church and American democracy; but I must always honour the Confucianist ethos. Even now, I can find life confusing.)

This childish desire to be someone else and to be somewhere else seemed to have nurtured in me a genuine fever to be on the move, counterbalanced by the need to have the security of a home. (Nothing speaks of this paradoxical state of mind better than someone who travels and moves a lot with thousands of books as part of her possession.) I have since lived a peripatetic life, both in reality and in my mind. As a child, I wanted to leave Hong Kong. Regular visits to Macau were not enough. For two decades, I lived in Vancouver and had moved home

twelve times, thus fulfilling a childhood dream in many ways —
acquiring a university education, immersing in Western culture, living
in interesting accommodations, spending money on books. Now I teach
in southern Alberta and have a home there. I travel to Vancouver every
long weekend, Christmas, and the summer months. I take my laptop
and files with me when I stay for a longer period, so that I continue
my research and writing wherever I am. I travel to Asia and Europe
to give papers at conferences and to research. Once in a rare while
I would take a holiday that did not involve giving a paper at an
academic conference.

As I get older, each trip becomes more tiring. Flying has lost its
glamour. The long duration going anywhere has become tedious. But
each time after I have unpacked, I would start planning the next trip.
To keep travelling seems to be an important way to affirm my own
existence. The waiting lounge of any airport is a comforting space. If I
am not travelling to remind myself of who I am, or am not, then I do it
through writing.

Writing is not only essential to my profession. It sustains my
imagination. I don't mean imagination as in fiction writing, but
imagination as a person who participates intellectually in society, who
absorbs ideas and processes experiences. Mapping one's life and retracing
one's existence have various effects and serve several goals. As far as
my project is concerned, writing is an analytical process; writing about
my early years is a way to understand the person I am and am evolving
to be. Unlike conventional autobiographies of earlier times, penned by
great men (mainly) and occasionally women, my project isn't a
testimony to goodness and greatness. Unlike victim memoirs, mine
doesn't show that an individual can overcome obstacles to attain
achievements. It is, instead, my own investigation of affiliations I formed
and rejected in my childhood — familial, social, racial, religious.

I'd like to think that it is an affectionate portrait of a specific
cultural world full of anomalies, a world that does not exist anymore.
It is a way to acknowledge the benign and paradoxical influences in
my first twenty years — parents who shunned Western society but were
enamoured of Western education and religion; a convent education that

ensured that I grew up as an individual, in spite of its disciplinary nature; and cities that contrasted each other as colonial outposts, cities that have since influenced the ways I react to natural and urban landscapes.

This project is a belated love letter to my childhood, which was not without problems; and a love letter to the colonial cities of Macau and Hong Kong.

It is my way of explaining to myself why I didn't want a family. Childhood and parents — not always a successful combination. Disasters in parenting can be averted, yet one doesn't want to take the chance of ruining someone else's life. To show love is important — psychological analysis is not all hogwash. But if one learns not to be spontaneously affectionate, then one doesn't have the knack. Obviously some scars remain from disappointments and fears experienced in childhood. Each person deals with these experiences differently. Otherwise, the world would be a worse place than it is now. Or a better place.

My life pattern is seemingly a cliché of Chinese-American/Chinese-Canadian blueprint — cultural conflicts, mother/daughter conflicts, home/in-exile conflicts. But I experienced a unique childhood. It made me a unique person.

Appendix: An Academic Insertion

Begin at the beginning. That was my plan when I first started drafting the structure of my autobiography. State one's name, one's birth date and place, one's parents' names, and so on. This narrative plan would provide forensic clarity as well as the illusion of truthfulness. However, it also simplifies the process of subjectivity-formation and precludes the equally messy reality of one's memories and the representations of these memories on paper. If I should begin my autobiography with my birth, or perhaps my parents', or even my grandparents', followed by annual events, school, love affairs, marriages, professional achievements, and so on, I would have fallen into a pattern of inscribing subjectivity that privileges a male tradition of telling one's story, a tradition that promises a logical resolution to the puzzlement of existence, and an affirmation of the enlightenment ideals. But this linear progression is a narrative that bears no resemblance to the constantly shifting perspectives that present themselves as one reviews one's life and tries to make sense of events, of commissions and omissions, of departures and arrivals. It does not reflect the perpetual conflict between the nature of representing/writing and the nature of remembering. Neither does this narrative pattern sufficiently articulate the cultural pressures a Chinese woman experiences, nor adequately address the contradictory lives of what Rey Chow calls a "diasporic person in diaspora." If the postmodern subject is multiple and decentred, then the diasporic subject is even more so. To articulate its existence and reality, the diasporic writer needs to contend with not only the disconnect between meaning and words, but also with the many historical and social trajectories that constitute a diasporic subjectivity.

This autobiography project deals with my dual-colonial subjectivity, my claim to being a Han Chinese, an ethnic identity that reaches back several thousand years (even though the concept of what constitutes Han ethnicity has been much debated); and my allegiance to various languages: the vernacular Cantonese as a family language, the classical written Chinese script as a reading language amongst others, English as my written language. My religious upbringing was strongly Catholic; the family had been Catholic for three generations on my mother's side, an indication of my family's familiarity with Western mores. My cultural and ethical upbringing was Confucianist. Already, before I could find my own life script, I was a product of dominant life scripts grounded in history, in class, in gender, and in race. As a result, an ethnic Chinese diasporic woman academic could find that, even when given a voice, her native experiences remain "untranslatable," to gloss Rey Chow's term in *Writing Diaspora*.

The Chinese Confucianist culture and the Chinese language is a tradition of male domination. This tradition inflicts various limitations on a Chinese woman writing her autobiography. In the context of traditional Confucianism, I should come under the censure of my family as well as society at large. If I were to follow the path of a dutiful Chinese daughter brought up in the Confucianist tradition, I should not be writing about my family and its foibles and failings, nor should I be writing about myself, not being someone of historical or political importance, given that classical Chinese, as Wu Pei-Yi states, "is the perfect instrument for stating and restating the exemplary," and though "virtuous maidens and chaste widows" are mentioned in county records, numbering in the tens of thousands, "these good women [...] remain faceless and in most cases nameless, only identifiable by the surnames of their fathers or husbands." Not only am I positioning myself as a critic of the life that my parents had gifted me, I am writing my autobiography in English instead of the language of my ancestors. (Yet, the formality and tradition of classical Chinese question the legitimacy of a narrative that addresses not only an individual's life, but a woman's life.) As I bear my father's name, I would be expected to censor any details in my early life that reflect negatively on the Ng family, since "revealing one's own sins [and other personal experiences] in public ran against the grain of a culture [...] which put so much emphasis upon propriety and discretion" (Wu). (But to present a whitewashed account would negate one of the presumed purposes of the genre of life writing.) If in the autobiography I analyze and criticize my parents, it would be an act of filial impiety. (But literature bears many examples of critiques of problematic familial relationships.) Thus, as a woman brought up by traditional Chinese parents, writing my autobiography is an act of cultural defiance.

Even when I have overcome the patriarchal Confucianist tradition and refused to be silent and wise, writing about my family and my personal relationships in Hong Kong involves navigating the disconnect amongst the various languages in my mind. As Wu explains, "The Chinese writing system, consisting of characters rather than phonetic notations, had determined from the very beginning that in its written form the language was to be used to record facts [...] rather than to transcribe speech verbatim." Classical or written Chinese is not a language that facilitates expressions of individual emotions and psychological conflicts; English is a more fluent language for me to express life. Yet, though I am writing my autobiography in English, my memories are constructed of situations and conversations performed in Cantonese, and my knowledge of Chinese history and literature is through formalized written Chinese. After I have translated my memories and knowledge into an English that is suitable for the genre and for publication, it becomes a life lived in three languages compressed into one.

Thus far, I have to decide to forgo Confucianist reticence and write about personal matters; I also have to overcome the innate linguistic confusion of remembering in Cantonese and classical Chinese, then translating memories into English. Most of all, I want to write in an English that is not an obvious translation of the Chinese and is different from the emotionalism in writings by famous modern Chinese writers such as Bing Xin, Ding Ling, and others. I have to make a rhetorical choice. Traditional Chinese women autobiographies in the May Fourth era is a genre that, as Lingzhen Wang notes, "has often been viewed as representing insignificant life experience, transmitting self-indulgent voices, and lacking broad social scale and objectivity." By implication, male writers write of significant life experience in an objective voice, thus providing the reading public with narratives of social relevance. However, even as I disagree with this patronizing view of modern Chinese women writing, and even as I have chosen to resist Confucianist patriarchal tradition, I remain under the influence, on the one hand, of Chinese prejudice against individual self-expressions, and on the other hand, of the analytical Western tradition that privileges objectivity over subjectivity.

So far the conflicts involved in recalling and recounting my early life are grounded in ethnic and linguistic contexts. A more specific conflict originates from my education. The convent education of Western enlightenment did more than teach me to control emotional indulgence in writing. Even as my mother was rigorous in educating me to become a good daughter and an eventual good wife, I found another set of female role models in the Catholic nuns at Maryknoll, an American missionary order. At home, I had a strict, traditional Chinese mother against whom I rebelled. At school, I had educated, encouraging, forgiving mothers. How should I write about these various mother figures, on some of whom I developed adolescent crushes? How do I extricate the sense of sin and damnation and atonement a Catholic education inculcated from the sunny and happy memories I have of learning, of getting good marks, of being the teacher's pet? Accounts I have read of convent educations usually suggest a regime of disciplinary oppression, of Western domination, of religious intolerance. For instance, Karen Armstrong writes of her harrowing experience being trained as a postulant in 1962 "along the old lines of severe Victorian discipline" even as The Second Vatican Council was meeting in Rome. Eventually, her study of English literature liberated her from the prison house of the convent.

In contrast, my convent education liberated me from the prison house of Confucianist and traditional Chinese disciplines; it liberated me from thinking and values that I was already rebelling against. My convent upbringing gave me autonomy. In a recent UNICEF report, a child's sense of educational well-being is rated as one of six categories essential in the child's upbringing (Westcott). I rate my educational well-being very high, while I would be more critical of my family and peer relationships, another category listed in the report. It is true that the Maryknoll nuns had acculturated me to Western art, Western literature, and Western values so thoroughly that I became a stranger in feelings and thoughts to my parents. But I didn't and still don't think of my convent education as a form of imperialistic domination. Otherwise, my many fellow students would also have rejected Chinese culture and become thoroughly acculturated in Western aesthetics and values, which was certainly not the case. I have to find a "balanced" way to represent these formative years while writing against the grain. My ambivalent attitude towards the history of British colonialism in Hong Kong also makes me ask myself if I am still "working in anti-imperialist discourse," as Rey Chow categorizes postcolonial critics in *Writing Diaspora*.

If I were writing this autobiography in the 70s, while I was still a teenager in Hong Kong, my experience of colonialism would have been very differently expressed. Certainly I remember racialized treatment and the social tension between the non-Chinese and the majority Chinese population in Hong Kong. But colonial relationships are mediated through class. The working class and the labourers in Hong Kong, who lived well away from the small and exclusive neighbourhoods of the expatriates, had very little knowledge or contact with their colonizers, unless they were working as servants. Even the middle class, to which my family belonged, had very little to do with the Western colonial presence. We had no Western friends; we socialized only with Chinese by choice; and if our friends and relatives were oppressed, they were oppressed by their Chinese employers, by their greedy Chinese landlords and others in the social structure. One could say that the wealthy and the powerful Chinese were always friendly with the colonial authority; hence colonial oppression was maintained through the economic system. But, one could also say that some wealthy and powerful Chinese had very little regards for the poor Chinese. In a city so motivated by commerce, the stock market, land development, and so on, race could at times be less important than one's bank account, the car one drives, the number of servants one can afford. As I was growing up, I was far more aware of which stratum of social class my family belonged to than what race. Thus, the first Western friend I knew was rejected totally by my mother, not only because of race, but also because of class. My mother's outright rejection of interracial relationships and her willing embrace of the Catholic Church and its Western representatives (nuns, priests, the Pope) is an example of the paradox inherent in the colonial culture of Hong Kong, and illustrates a kind of cultural pragmatism that most Hong Kong Chinese practised, consciously or subconsciously. A Westerner without money was not desirable; but powerful Western religious institutions were acceptable, especially when they provided the children with a solid education.

However, now that I am making my living as an academic working in anti-imperialist discourse, my perspective has changed and my recounting of my life under colonial rule also requires a different narrative voice than the one I would have used regarding my convent education. Edward Said's *Out of Place* and Shirley Lim's *Among the White Moon Faces* offer two examples of autobiographies written by postcolonial critics. These accounts are worthy examples, both of the genre of autobiography and of the academic profession. *Simplified,* they are narratives of oppressed individuals who overcame economic, or political, or psychological obstacles within a specific historical context. Not only did these individuals refuse to succumb to the system; they become resistant fighters against the colonial system through their teaching and writing. These narratives are "victim" memoirs with a triumphant ending.

I admire these memoirs. But Said's colonized Cairo and Lim's colonized Malaysia are not the same political constructs as my colonized Hong Kong. As an individual, I was not victimized by the colonial system. If I were writing about Hong Kong and Chinese culture in general, I would resort to my postcolonial voice: the colonial system had suppressed Chinese autonomy; it had exploited Chinese labour and land; British colonialists, with their attitude of racial superiority, had treated Chinese with contempt; exclusive enclaves, such as tennis and cricket clubs, had made Chinese presence unwelcome; there were never equal social interactions between the British and the Chinese. (Although not many Chinese of our social circles would want to have any interactions with the Brits either.) But if I were writing about myself, the obstacles I had to overcome were imposed by my own culture, which I consider anti-woman and anti-individual; and because my relatives and social circles eschewed contact with Westerners, I consider them xenophobic. Yet I don't want to write an autobiography of nostalgia for the good old days of colonialism. My personal narrative needs to be contextualized within the global phenomenon of postcolonial movements. I have to find the rhetoric space that intersects the personal specifics and the cultural/historical. Perhaps my representation of an experienced colonial culture is closer to Michael Ondaatje's in *Running in the Family*.

In her essay on Michael Ondaatje in *Writing the Roaming Subject: The Biotext in Canadian Literature*, Joanne Saul attributes "the elegiac tone of much of the book" to the numerous ruptures and gaps in Ondaatje's search for connection and belonging. I add uneasy nostalgia to the causes for Ondaatje's elegy to a colonial culture. A colonized subject has to tread carefully when writing nostalgically of a colonized past — the voice of Frantz Fanon echoes as a warning bell. Like Ondaatje, I want to represent my own, and by extension, my family's experience of a colonial culture not as one of political opposition and struggle, but of acceptance, compliance even. More importantly, Hong Kong culture, as distinct from the colonial culture of Malaya and Ceylon, was a colonized culture that was forcefully mediated by the neighbouring presence of China. Furthermore, unlike the Malay Chinese, the Hong Kong Chinese constituted the majority. These Chinese practised with pride their culture and customs, with little intervention from the colonial power. As a matter of fact, to imply a strong political awareness of and hostility towards British colonialism in Hong Kong in the 50s and 60s would be inaccurate.

Yet, I am also aware of the fact that there are critics, like Saul, who believe that "'responsible' immigrant narratives should represent or be faithful to history; that they should engage with the structures of power; and that 'visible' minority writers should not only be 'original' but also 'authentic'." It is a critical position that I am familiar with in Postcolonial Studies; I myself have advocated an ethical representation in fiction that features ethnic minorities. However, while the theoretical position argues for a general policy towards ethnic representation, my own autobiography has to do with an individual lived experience. This conflict between representation and the politics of reading argues for a contextual and nuanced culture of critical interpretation.

Similar to Ondaatje in *Running in the Family*, I want to evoke a landscape of tropical heat, lush landscape, blue sky merging with blue water, colonial architecture, and the multiple contact/non-contact zones between the West and the East. I want to write about the suddenness of monsoon rainstorms, the brilliant greenness of the palm fronds, the pervasive smell of frangipani in the summer, or the shapely silhouettes of women in cheongsams. My mother and I rode in rickshaw when I was a child. I was eight and was on the same cross-harbour ferry when a scene from *The World of Susie Wong* was shot, a film that the family both enjoyed and laughed at. This was the culture I grew up in, the culture that nurtured me. Yet, this descriptive approach could be critiqued as a "tendency to exoticize" (Saul). But if I were writing a realistic description of my childhood — not embellished with literary conceits, not conjured out of picture books or plagiarized from travel narratives; in other words, not an orientalist exercise — would it still be a form of exoticism, just because the Hong Kong weather is different from a Canadian winter or the cultural practices are different from those in a Canadian suburbia?

The more I write, the more apparent it becomes that no one particular narrative strategy would work for me, certainly not "the kind of coming-to-voice narrative that relies on a unified concept of the ethnic subject and a developmental narrative of assimilation or belonging" (Saul). My autobiography project is intellectually facilitated by my identity as a Canadian ethnic woman academic and the academic culture in the 90s that nurtured me. Shirley Neuman's contribution on life writing in *Literary History of Canada* and other critics writing on autobiography as a "serious" literary genre (Saul); the inclusion of ethnic writers and their works within recognized area studies such as English; the distinctly different configuration of ethnic identities within the context of multiculturalism in Canada, all form a productive backdrop for me, as well as for other writers with ethnic backgrounds, to explore the ambiguities of belonging and of identity (Saul). Even as I write about a colonized past, my memories are informed by a postcolonial present. In *Writing Diaspora*, Rey Chow claims that "the goal of 'writing diaspora' is [...] to unlearn that submission to one's ethnicity such as

'Chineseness' as the ultimate signified even as one continues to support movements for democracy and human rights in China, Hong Kong, and elsewhere." Chow's position is deeply connected to her identity as a Hong Kong Chinese growing up in the 60s and 70s, and to be a Chinese in Hong Kong during that period, when China was undergoing the turmoil of the Cultural Revolution and the United States the turmoil of the Vietnam War and the counterculture movements, was to be a Chinese caught in the matrix of conflicting and feuding cultural ideologies. Like Chow, I also nurture simultaneous affiliation for and resistance against the centrism of Chineseness and the eurocentrism of the West.

This borderland anxiety pursued me throughout my writing this book. "How should I position myself?" was a constant question. As a matter of fact, I have no other viable position from which I can narrate except as someone in diaspora. I am no longer a colonized subject. I am not in a postcolonial condition, having left Hong Kong and accepted Canadian citizenship. But, unlike Chinese Canadians whose ancestors settled in Canada in the nineteenth century, I am still affiliated to Hong Kong, although a Hong Kong that now belongs to China, whose official language of Putonghua I cannot speak and whose cultural ambassadors would have indexed me as a "Westernized Chinese woman from colonial Hong Kong, this cultural bastard" (Chow). Thus, I can say that I now suffer the same chauvinistic discrimination that other expatriate Chinese have experienced. Yet, rather than feeling abashed as a serial non-belonger — not China-Chinese, not Hong Konger, not local-born Canadian, not Portuguese-speaking Macanese, I revel in this multiplicity of non-identities as the eventual norm of social identity of people around the world.

Works Cited

All references made to external materials in the Preface, Introduction, and Academic Insertion have been cited from the following. Referenced page numbers are listed, in order of their appearance in the text, at the end of each entry.

Ang, Ien. *On Not Speaking Chinese: Living Between Asia and the West*. London: Routledge, 2001. (164, 172, 164).

Armstrong, Karen. *Through the Narrow Gate: A Memoir of Life In and Out of the Convent*. Toronto: Vintage, 2005. (72).

Barbour, John D. "Judging and Not Judging Parents." *The Ethics of Life Writing*. Ed. Paul John Eakin. Ithaca: Cornell UP, 2004. 73–98. (74).

Buss, Helen M. *Mapping Our Selves*. Montreal: McGill-Queen's UP, 1993. (189).

Chow, Rey. *Writing Diaspora. Tactics of Intervention in Contemporary Cultural Studies*. Bloomington and Indianapolis: Indiana UP, 1993. (23, 38, 53, 25, 26).

Couser, G. Thomas. *Vulnerable Subjects: Ethics and Life Writing*. Ithaca: Cornell UP, 2004. (x, x).

Manzoor, Sarfraz. "When Art Imitates Life." Accessed Feb 18, 3007. http://www.guardian.co.uk/commentisfree/2007/feb/17/comment. biography

Ng, Maria N. "Abusive Mothers: Literary Representations of the Mother Figure in Three Ethnic Chinese Writers — Hsieh Ping-ying, Denise Chong, and Chen Ying." *Asian Women: Interconnections*. Eds. Tineke Hellwig and Sunera Thobani. Toronto: Canadian Scholars, 2006. 139–60. (139–40, 141).

Saul, Joanne. *Writing the Roaming Subject: The Biotext in Canadian Literature*. Toronto: U of Toronto P, 2006. (53, 36, 52, 37, 4–5, 6).

Titley, Brian. "Heil Mary: Magdalen Asylums and Moral Regulation in Ireland." *History of Education Review* 35.2 (2006): 1-15. (1)

Wang, Lingzhen. *Personal Matters: Women's Autobiographical Practice in Twentieth-Century China*. Stanford: Stanford UP, 2004. (2).

Westcott, Kathryn. "Why are Dutch children so happy?" *BBC News.* Accessed Feb 18, 2007. http://newsote.bbc.co.uk/pagetools/print/ news.bbc.co.uk/2/hi/europe/

Wu, Pei-yi. *The Confucian's Progress. Autobiographical Writings in Traditional China.* Princeton: Princeton UP, 1990. (12, 216, 11).